Lizzie's
Amish Cookbook
Favorite recipes from three generations of Amish cooks!

Lizzie's
Amish Cookbook

Favorite recipes from three generations of Amish cooks!

LINDA BYLER
with LAURA ANN LAPP *(Linda's daughter)*
and ANNA KAUFFMAN *(Linda's mother)*

Good Books

New York, New York

Lizzie's Amish Cookbook includes excerpts from:
Running Around (and Such), When Strawberries Bloom,
and Big Decisions, the three books by Linda Byler in the
"Lizzie Searches for Love" series.

The Bible passages are from the King James Version of the
Bible.

Cover design by Koechel Peterson & Associates, Inc.,
Minneapolis, Minnesota

Illustrations throughout the book by Cheryl Benner

Design by Cliff Snyder

LIZZIE'S AMISH COOKBOOK
Copyright © 2011 by Good Books, an imprint of Skyhorse Publishing, Inc.
ISBN: 978-1-56148-735-6 (paperback edition)
ISBN: 978-1-56148-738-7 (comb-bound paperback edition)
Library of Congress Catalog Card Number: 2011034142

Good Books books may be purchased in bulk at special discounts for sales
promotion, corporate gifts, fund-raising, or educational purposes. Special
editions can also be created to specifications. For details, contact the Special
Sales Department, Good Books, 307 West 36th Street, 11th Floor, New York,
NY 10018 or info@skyhorsepublishing.com.

Good Books in an imprint of Skyhorse Publishing, Inc.®,
a Delaware corporation.

Visit our website at www.goodbooks.com.

10 9 8 7 6 5 4 3 2

Library of Congress Cataloging-in-Publication Data
Byler, Linda.
Lizzie's Amish cookbook : favorite recipes from three generations of
Amish cooks! / Linda Byler.
    p. cm.
Includes index.
ISBN 978-1-56148-735-6 (pbk. : alk. paper) -- ISBN 978-1-56148-738-7
(comb-bound : alk. paper) 1. Amish cooking. 2. Cookbooks. I. Title.
TX721.B955 2011
641.5'66--dc23   2011034142

Printed in the United States of America

Table of Contents

Table Prayer

Enable us to use Thy manifold blessings
with moderation:

Grant our hearts wisdom to avoid excess

In eating and drinking

And in the cares of this life:

Teach us to put our trust in Thee

And to await Thy helping hand.

TRADITIONAL AMISH PRAYER

A Word About These Recipes

Food wraps through, in, and around Amish social occasions—from Sunday church lunches to neighborhood work parties. Food secures these families. It builds bonds in the Amish faith community. It adds pure pleasure to the lives of these disciplined people—first and foremost among them, Lizzie Glick.

Lizzie is the lead character in the three "Lizzie Searches for Love" novels: *Running Around (and Such)*, Book One; *When Strawberries Bloom*, Book Two; and *Big Decisions*, Book Three. You'll find excerpts from these tender stories among the recipes in this Cookbook.

Food is, without a doubt, Lizzie's love.

When she isn't eating, she's anticipating food. When she packs her lunch, she puts in an extra whoopie pie, just in case. When she thinks ahead to Sunday supper with her gang of friends, she hopes for homemade pizza as fervently as she hopes to catch Stephen's eye.

Food is Lizzie's comfort and her entertainment. Food is Lizzie's reward after her first morning as a *maud* and after Mam finally began to return to health.

These are novelist Linda Byler's mother's own recipes, gathered and written down by Linda's daughter, Laura Lapp.

Make them yourself and you'll quickly see why Lizzie loves to eat, whether at a school picnic, at Emma's and Mandy's weddings, or of course, at Mommy Glick's table.

Before she could ask Mam more about God's will and future husbands, Mommy Glick called them to dinner. Lizzie followed Mam into the dining room where the table was covered with food.

Mommy Glick had made chicken potpie with large chunks of potatoes swimming in thick chicken gravy. Chunks of white chicken meat were mixed with the potpie squares and sprinkled with bright green parsley. Mommy Glick made her own noodles, too. She mixed egg yolks with flour, and the potpie turned out thick and yellow and chewy. It was the best thing ever to eat with creamy chicken gravy.

Lizzie also admired the baked beans that had been baking most of the forenoon and now were rich with tomato sauce and bacon. Bits of onion floated among the beans, and steam wafted from the granite roaster. Applesauce, dark green sweet pickles, and red beet eggs completed the meal.

Lizzie was so hungry she forgot all about her diet for the day. When they finished eating the main part of the meal, Lizzie and Mandy helped themselves to pieces of shoofly pie and sat on the steps of the porch together. They each bit off the very tips of their pieces.

"No one else in the whole world can make shoofly pies like Mommy Glick," Lizzie said.

Mandy nodded, her mouth full as she ate her way through the whole delicious piece.

RUNNING AROUND (AND SUCH)

*He causeth the grass to
grow for the cattle,*

*and herb for the service
of man:*

*that he may bring forth
food out of the earth;*

PSALM 104:14

6

Breads and Spreads

Becky Zook Bread

Makes 5 loaves
Prep Time: 30 minutes
Rising Time: 2-4 hours • *Baking Time: 30-40 minutes*

4 cups warm (110-112°) water, *divided*

½ Tbsp. dry, active yeast

½ cup and ½ Tbsp. sugar, *divided*

¼ cup lard, *or* Crisco, melted

1 Tbsp. salt

3 quarts Occident* flour

*Occident flour is bread flour made from western wheat.

1. In a small bowl, combine 1 cup water, yeast, and ½ Tbsp. sugar. Stir and let stand until bubbly, approximately 2-5 minutes.

2. In another large bowl, mix 3 cups water, ½ cup sugar, lard, and salt.

3. Pour yeast mixture into the large bowl and stir.

4. Using a spoon, beat in flour until too thick to stir. Then, use hands to mix in remaining flour.

5. Knead bread dough until smooth and elastic.

6. Cover with towel or plastic wrap and set in a warm place to rise. Let rise for 1 hour, or until dough doubles in size.

7. Using fists, punch dough down and remove from bowl.

8. Shape dough into 5 loaves.

9. Place loaves into well-greased loaf pans and let rise for 1 hour, covered, or until dough doubles in size.

10. Bake at 350° for 30-40 minutes.

TIP:

To check if the bread is finished, tap the top. Bread is ready when you hear a dull sound.

Wasn't that just so Emma-ish? Planning all her cozy housewife duties a year or so in advance. She still loved old houses with homemade quilts and rag rugs, and baking bread and jelly rolls, and all sorts of other impossible things.

"I'm not going to help," Lizzie announced loudly, pulling out another forkful of cake.

Mam kept washing dishes and without turning her head, said, "Oh, yes, you are."

RUNNING AROUND (AND SUCH)

Refrigerator Bread

Makes 2 loaves

Prep Time: 30 minutes

Rising Time: 2-4 hours • Baking Time: 30 minutes

2 pkgs., *or* 2 Tbsp., dry, active yeast

2 cups warm (110-112°) water

½ cup sugar

⅓ cup oil

1 egg, beaten

6½-7 cups flour

1 tsp. salt

1. In large bowl, dissolve yeast in warm water. Let stand until foamy, approximately 2-5 minutes.

2. Stir in sugar and oil.

3. Add egg, flour, and salt. Knead dough until smooth and elastic.

4. Place dough in a greased bowl. Cover and let rise 1-2 hours, or until double in size.

5. With fists, punch down dough.

6. Place dough in well-greased loaf pans.

7. Cover. Let rise for 1-2 hours, or until nearly doubled in size.

8. Bake at 350° for 30 minutes.

After punching down dough, place covered bowl of dough in refrigerator. Take out fresh bread dough as needed to make bread or rolls. When using dough from refrigerator, allow at least 2-3 hours for dough to warm up and rise before baking.

> *At lunchtime, Dat would spread butter on a thick slice of homemade bread, sprinkle salt beside his plate until he had made a little pile, then select a spring onion. He would dip the onion in the salt, bite it off and quickly take a bite of the buttered bread, and then chew the two together.*
>
> RUNNING AROUND (AND SUCH)

Whole Wheat Bread

Makes 3 loaves

Prep Time: 30 minutes • Standing Time: 1 hour
Rising Time: 2-4 hours • Baking Time: 35 minutes

2½ Tbsp. dry, active yeast

2½ cups warm (110-112°) water, *divided*

1 Tbsp. sugar

4 tsp. salt

2 cups whole wheat flour

½ cup brown sugar

½ cup water

½ cup oil, *or* lard, melted

½ cup molasses, *or* honey

4-5 cups white flour

1. In large bowl, dissolve yeast in 2 cups water.

2. Add sugar, salt, and whole wheat flour. Mix well.

3. Let stand for 1 hour.

4. Add brown sugar, ½ cup water, oil, and molasses. Stir together.

5. Add white flour until dough is smooth and elastic.

6. Cover with towel or plastic wrap and let rise for 1 hour, or until dough is double in size.

7. With fists, punch down dough.

8. Shape dough into 3 loaves and place in well-greased loaf pans.

9. Cover. Let dough rise for 1 hour, or until dough is double in size.

10. Bake at 350° for 35 minutes.

TIP:

For faster rising time, place the covered bowl in the oven. Keep oven off. The warmth of the pilot light helps dough rise faster.

> *Emma's eyes lit up, and she hurried back to the pantry. "Look at this," she said, holding a perfect loaf of homemade bread. It looked exactly like the loaf of bread in the children's book about the Little Red Hen who baked a beautiful loaf of bread with the wheat she raised.*
>
> BIG DECISIONS

Oatmeal Bread

Makes 3 loaves
Prep Time: 30 minutes
Rising Time: 2-4 hours • *Baking Time: 30 minutes*

2 cups boiling water

1 cup dry quick oats

½ cup whole wheat flour

½ cup brown sugar

1 Tbsp. salt

¼ stick (2 Tbsp.) butter, softened

1 Tbsp. dry, active yeast

½ cup very warm (110-115°) water

5 cups all-purpose flour

melted butter

1. In large bowl, pour 2 cups boiling water over dry oatmeal.

2. Stir in whole wheat flour, sugar, salt, and butter.

3. Allow to cool.

4. In a separate bowl, dissolve yeast in ½ cup very warm water.

5. Add yeast to oatmeal mixture.

6. Add all-purpose flour and beat until creamy.

7. Knead dough until smooth and elastic.

8. Cover dough with towel or plastic wrap, and let rise for 1 hour.

9. With fists, punch down dough.

10. Shape into 3 loaves and put into well-greased loaf pans.

11. Cover. Allow dough to rise for 1 hour, or until dough has doubled in size.

12. Bake at 350° for 30 minutes.

13. When done baking, brush tops of loaves with melted butter.

Alongside was a thick slice of homemade oatmeal bread and a small dish with a pat of bright yellow butter made from the cream of their own cow. There was also a small glass dish of golden honey from the midwives' own beehives down by their orchard, which Lizzie thought was simply the most extraordinary thing she had ever heard of.

She would ask Stephen to get a few hives of bees, and she would get the recipe to make this light, spongy, oatmeal bread. She had, quite simply, never been as inspired to eat healthy things and grow them in her own backyard as she was now with this supper tray.

BIG DECISIONS

Potato Rolls

Makes 12 rolls
Prep Time: 30 minutes
Rising Time: 3-3½ hours • Baking Time: 15-20 minutes

1 cup warm (110-112°) water

1 Tbsp. dry, active yeast

½ cup oil

1 cup mashed potatoes

½ cup sugar

2 eggs

½ tsp. salt

5-5½ cups Occident,* or all-purpose, flour

*Occident flour is bread flour made from western wheat.

1. In small bowl, mix together water and yeast.

2. Let stand 15 minutes.

3. In a large bowl, stir together oil, mashed potatoes, sugar, eggs, and salt.

4. Add yeast mixture.

5. Stir in flour and knead until smooth. Dough will be sticky.

6. Cover and let rise for 2 hours.

7. Using hands, shape dough into rolls.

8. Place in well-greased cake pan or cupcake pan. Cover. Let rise 1-1½ hours, or until dough has doubled in size.

9. Bake at 350° until rolls are golden brown, about 15-20 minutes.

> *"Do you want to have sloppy-looking pieces of thread sticking out of your neckline or from under your cape on your very first weekend?"* Emma shouted.
>
> *Lizzie narrowed her eyes, considering. "No-o-o."*
>
> *"Okay, then settle down and watch me turn this knob. You have to stay on the edge of the fabric. You can't just zigzag anywhere you feel like."*
>
> *Lizzie's sigh of resignation assured Mam that she was well on the way to learning how to sew, so she relaxed as she started a batch of homemade bread. Susan and KatieAnn pushed their chairs up to the kitchen cabinets. Mam let them stir the yeast into the water, her heart melting as it always did when they wanted to be her helpers.*
>
> RUNNING AROUND (AND SUCH)

Dinner Rolls

Makes 12-18 rolls

Prep Time: 30 minutes • Cooling Time: 30-45 minutes
Rising Time: 2-4 hours • Baking Time: 20-30 minutes

2 Tbsp. dry, active yeast

½ cup warm (110-112°) water

1 cup scalded milk

1 Tbsp. salt

½ cup sugar

1 stick (8 Tbsp.) butter, melted

2 eggs, beaten

5½ cups flour, *divided*

Melted butter for top

1. Dissolve yeast in warm water and let stand.

2. In medium pan, heat milk until almost boiling.

3. Add salt, sugar, and butter to milk.

4. Cool milk mixture until lukewarm, 80-85°.

5. Stir in yeast mixture and eggs.

6. Add flour, stirring in as much as you can until well mixed.

7. Knead in remaining flour, or as much as you can, until dough is smooth and elastic.

8. Place dough in well-greased bowl. Cover and let rise 1-2 hours, or until dough is double in size.

9. Form dough into rolls and place on well-greased cookie sheet or jelly-roll pan, approximately 2" apart.

10. Cover. Allow dough to rise 1-2 hours, or until dough is double in size.

11. Bake at 350° for 20-30 minutes, until rolls are light brown.

12. Brush tops of rolls with melted butter before taking off cookie sheet.

Every day at lunch, they sat beneath the oak tree in the soft fragrant grass and shared the food they had packed. Dora's mother made soft, light-as-a-feather dinner rolls, which melted in Lizzie's mouth.

RUNNING AROUND (AND SUCH)

Quick Cinnamon Rolls

Makes 2 large pans
Prep Time: 20-40 minutes
Rising Time: 30-60 minutes • Baking Time: 25-35 minutes

Prepared bread dough, enough to make 2 loaves

Butter at room temperature

Cinnamon

Sauce:

1 cup cream

1 cup corn syrup

½ cup honey

1½ cups brown sugar

1 stick (8 Tbsp.) butter

1. Roll out bread dough ¼"-½" thick.

2. Spread dough with butter and sprinkle with cinnamon.

3. Starting with long side, roll up dough.

4. Slice rolled dough into pieces about 1" thick.

5. Place sliced dough into well-greased baking pans. Cover and let rise ½-1 hour, or until dough has doubled in size.

6. Bake at 350° for 20-30 minutes until golden brown on top.

7. To make sauce, boil cream, corn syrup, honey, brown sugar, and butter for 5 minutes.

8. When cinnamon rolls are finished baking, pour sauce over rolls in pans.

9. Return to oven for 5 minutes.

10. Serve warm.

TIP:
_____

Refrigerator Bread works well for these rolls (see page 10).

> *The evening Stephen and Lizzie decided to seed the lawn turned into a fun-filled, festive evening. First, everyone raked the soil until it was fine and smooth, removing small rocks and leveling uneven hills of dirt. Dat and Jason arrived with their own rakes, Mam brought homemade cinnamon rolls, and they all worked on the new lawn, moving along the front of the house, down the opposite side of the driveway, and all along the sides and back of the house.*
>
> BIG DECISIONS

Cinnamon Rolls

Makes 4-5 round cake pans full

Prep Time: 45-60 minutes • Cooling Time: 30-45 minutes
Rising Time: 2-3½ hours • Baking Time: 15-20 minutes

1½ cups milk

2 sticks (16 Tbsp.) butter, cut in chunks

1 cup warm (110-112°) water

4 Tbsp. dry, active yeast

½ cup sugar

4 eggs, beaten

2 tsp. salt

8 cups flour, *divided*

Topping:

2 sticks (16 Tbsp.) butter, melted

½ cup brown sugar

1-2 tsp. cinnamon

1. In large saucepan, heat milk until almost boiling.

2. Stir in butter until dissolved.

3. Cool until lukewarm, 80-85°.

4. When cooled, add water, yeast, sugar, eggs, and salt.

5. Beat in 1-3 cups of flour.

6. Add rest of flour, kneading well.

7. Cover and let rise until doubled, 1-1½ hours.

8. Roll out dough to approximately ½" thick.

9. Brush with melted butter. Sprinkle with brown sugar and cinnamon.

10. Starting with the long side, roll up dough.

11. Cut the dough into slices that are 1" thick.

12. Place cut dough in well-greased pan and allow to rise for 1-2 hours or until double in size.

13. Bake at 350° until golden brown, about 15-20 minutes.

14. Cool slightly, but frost while still warm (see Frosting for Cinnamon Rolls, page 24).

Frosting for Cinnamon Rolls

Makes enough for 5 cake pans of Rolls
Prep Time: 15 minutes

1 stick (8 Tbsp.) plus 1 Tbsp.
butter, softened

4½ cups confectioners sugar

3 Tbsp. cream, *or* milk

1½ tsp. vanilla

1. Beat butter until smooth.

2. Cream in sugar, by hand or electric mixer.

3. When smooth, stir in cream or milk and vanilla, beating until creamy.

4. Spread over warm Cinnamon Rolls (see page 22).

Lizzie washed her hands well, made coffee, mixed iced tea, and then served a good snack. They all sat around the table, enjoying each other's company and Mam's delicious cinnamon rolls.

BIG DECISIONS

Banana Nut Bread

Makes 2 loaves

Prep Time: 15 minutes • *Baking Time: 45 minutes*

1 cup sugar

1 stick (8 Tbsp.) butter, softened

2 eggs

3 bananas, mashed

2 cups flour

1 tsp. baking soda

½ cup chopped nuts

1. In medium bowl, cream together sugar and butter.

2. Add eggs and beat well.

3. Using a fork, mash bananas and add to mixture.

4. Add flour, baking soda, and chopped nuts. Stir well.

5. Pour batter into 2 well-greased loaf pans.

6. Bake at 350° for about 45 minutes, or until toothpick inserted into center comes out clean.

Pumpkin Bread

Makes 2 loaves
Prep Time: 15 minutes • Baking Time: 1 hour

3 cups sugar
1 cup oil
4 eggs
2 cups pumpkin
3½ cups flour
1 tsp. baking powder
1 tsp. baking soda
1 tsp. salt
½ tsp. cloves
1 tsp. cinnamon
1 tsp. nutmeg
⅔ cup water

1. In a medium bowl, combine sugar, oil, eggs, and pumpkin.

2. In a separate bowl, combine flour, baking powder, baking soda, salt, cloves, cinnamon, and nutmeg.

3. Add dry ingredients to sugar mixture. Stir well.

4. Add water and stir to combine.

5. Pour batter into 2 well-greased loaf pans.

6. Bake at 350° for approximately 1 hour, or until toothpick inserted in center of loaves comes out clean.

TIP:

Always check bread before time is up. Bread may be done sooner than 1 hour.

Zucchini Bread

Makes 2 loaves
Prep Time: 15 minutes • Baking Time: 1 hour

3 eggs
2 cups sugar
1 cup oil
2 cups grated zucchini
1 Tbsp. vanilla
1 tsp. salt
1 Tbsp. cinnamon
1 tsp. baking soda
¼ tsp. baking powder
3 cups flour
1 cup chopped nuts,
optional

1. In a large bowl, combine eggs, sugar, and oil.

2. Stir in zucchini.

3. Add remaining ingredients in order given, except nuts. Stir well.

4. Add nuts if you wish.

5. Pour batter into 2 well-greased loaf pans.

6. Bake at 325° for 1 hour, or until toothpick inserted in center of loaves comes out clean.

7. Cool before removing from pan.

TIP:

If zucchini is big and has tough skin, peel before grating. If using young, slender zucchini, there is no need to peel.

Church
Peanut Butter
Marshmallow
Spread

Makes about 6 gallons spread
Prep Time: 15 minutes
Cooking Time: 15 minutes • Cooling Time: 3-4 hours

8 cups dark
brown sugar

4 cups water

½ cup light corn
syrup

6 pounds creamy
peanut butter

3 18-oz. jars
marshmallow crème

1. Mix brown sugar, water, and corn syrup together in a large stockpot.

2. Bring to a boil, stirring frequently to prevent sticking.

3. Remove from heat and cool completely.

4. In a separate bowl, combine peanut butter and marshmallow crème.

5. Carefully stir peanut-butter mixture into brown-sugar syrup.

6. Serve on fresh homemade bread.

This sweet and creamy spread is used in some communities for the lunch following church on Sunday.

This quantity may allow for leftovers for snacks during the week.

> *"That is just a great idea," Lizzie said. "Tell you what! The day of the hike, we'll ask permission to roast hot dogs and marshmallows!"*
>
> *"Crackers and peanut butter!" shouted a fourth-grader, who instantly slunk down in his seat after receiving some lowered eyebrow looks from the upper-graders.*
>
> *"I love a burned marshmallow between Ritz crackers with peanut butter on them," Lizzie said, smiling to reassure him.*
>
> WHEN STRAWBERRIES BLOOM

Cheese Spread

Makes 1-2 quarts

Prep Time: 45-60 minutes • *Standing Time: 8 hours, or overnight*

5 pounds sliced American cheese, yellow *or* white

6¼ cups water

1½ -2 tsp. baking soda

1. Set cheese out until it is at room temperature.

2. Pour water into 8- or 10-quart kettle. Bring to a boil.

3. Turn burner off and drop slices of cheese into the water slice by slice.

4. Stir often until cheese is melted.

5. Add baking soda.

6. Let stand at room temperature for 8 hours, or overnight.

7. Refrigerate.

8. Serve with bread, or with hard or soft pretzels.

NOTE:
_____

Cheese Spread is served at the lunch following
Sunday church. Typically it's spread on slices of
bread. Any leftovers may be eaten with hard or
soft pretzels.

> *After services were over, Lizzie helped
> the other single girls carry trays of
> bread and pies, ham, soft cheese spread,
> pickles, and red beets to the long tables
> where the traditional Sunday dinner
> was served. She caught sight of Stephen
> standing on the other side of the room,
> laughing at something Uncle Marvin
> had said. Stephen smiled at her and
> Lizzie's heart sped up.*
>
> WHEN STRAWBERRIES BLOOM

Church
Peanut Butter

Makes 2½ quarts
Prep Time: 15 minutes

2 quarts King Syrup

1½ pints creamy peanut butter

1. Combine King Syrup and peanut butter.

2. Stir until creamy.

3. Serve on homemade bread or toast.

NOTE:

This is one of the staples of the traditional Sunday lunch, served by the host family after church.

Mam made all kinds of cookies and candy, too. Rice Krispie treats and chocolate-coated peanut butter crackers were Lizzie's favorites.

Lizzie and Mandy always worked very hard to clean the entire house for Christmas, while Mam baked and cooked in the kitchen. They didn't decorate the house because that would be too worldly. Sometimes Mam allowed a few red candles on the windowsill or a candle set in the middle of the table.

WHEN STRAWBERRIES BLOOM

Breakfast Dishes

Creamed Eggs

Makes 6-8 servings

Prep Time: 15 minutes • *Cooking Time: 5 minutes*

¼ stick (2 Tbsp.) butter

2 Tbsp. flour

1 tsp. salt

dash of black pepper

2 cups milk

6 hard-boiled eggs

6-8 slices toast

1. Melt butter in medium saucepan.

2. Stir in flour, salt, and pepper.

3. Stirring constantly, slowly add milk.

4. Cook until smooth and slightly thickened. Remove from heat.

5. Peel eggs. Slice or chop.

6. Stir into white sauce.

7. Serve over toast or cornmeal mush (see page 58).

TO HARD-BOIL EGGS:

1. Place eggs in saucepan. Cover with water.

2. Bring to a full, rolling boil.

3. Turn off burner.

4. With lid on, let eggs stand for 10 minutes.

5. Cool immediately under cold running water.

6. Peel and serve.

> *But she loved to eat eggs—fried, scrambled, soft-boiled, just any which way, with salt, pepper, or ketchup. They were delicious. Mam often made an egg in a nest for Jason. She began with a slice of bread, cut the center out of it with a small drinking glass, buttered the "frame" of bread on both sides, and then laid it on the griddle. She broke an egg into the hole in the center, then fried it until the bread was browned and the egg set.*
>
> *So Mam's chickens were a good thing, providing their family with fresh eggs every day, until egg production dropped drastically.*
>
> RUNNING AROUND (AND SUCH)

Dutch Eggs

Makes 8 servings

Prep Time: 15 minutes • Baking Time: 45 minutes

8 eggs
2½ cups milk
5 Tbsp. flour
½ tsp. baking powder
½-1 tsp. salt

1. In medium bowl, beat eggs and milk together.

2. Add flour, baking powder, and salt. Mix well.

3. Pour mixture into well-greased 2-quart casserole dish.

4. Bake at 350° for 45 minutes.

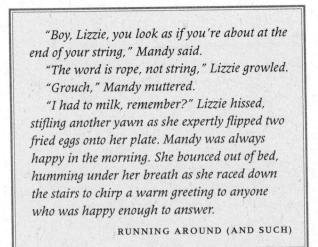

> "Boy, Lizzie, you look as if you're about at the end of your string," Mandy said.
>
> "The word is rope, not string," Lizzie growled.
>
> "Grouch," Mandy muttered.
>
> "I had to milk, remember?" Lizzie hissed, stifling another yawn as she expertly flipped two fried eggs onto her plate. Mandy was always happy in the morning. She bounced out of bed, humming under her breath as she raced down the stairs to chirp a warm greeting to anyone who was happy enough to answer.
>
> RUNNING AROUND (AND SUCH)

Fried Egg

Makes 1 serving

Prep Time: 1-2 minutes • Cooking Time: 4-5 minutes

2 tsp. butter	1. Place a small dab of butter in skillet or frying pan. Turn burner on high just until butter is melted.
egg	

2. Carefully break egg into pan. Turn heat down to medium-low.

3. When egg whites are set and white in color, turn the egg over gently, being careful not to break the yolk.

4. Fry for 1-2 minutes before serving.

> *Lizzie had put a spoonful of fried eggs and toast in her mouth so she couldn't answer.*
>
> *She was so hungry after her morning's work that she ate and ate without even thinking of calories or her weight.*
>
> RUNNING AROUND (AND SUCH)

Scrambled Eggs

Makes 4 servings

Prep Time: 3-5 minutes • *Cooking Time: 10 minutes*

4-5 eggs
¼ cup milk
¼-½ tsp. salt
dash of pepper
1-2 Tbsp. butter

1. In medium bowl, beat eggs.

2. Add milk, salt, and pepper. Beat with eggbeaters or wire whisk until frothy.

3. Melt butter in medium skillet.

4. Turn heat to medium-low and pour eggs into pan.

5. Stir or turn often so eggs don't stick to pan or get overdone.

6. Serve when eggs are nice and fluffy, after cooking for about 5-8 minutes.

VARIATION:

For creamy eggs, substitute 1 Tbsp. mayonnaise for 1 Tbsp. of milk.

"Not this spring, Mandy. Amish people have their weddings in the fall. In November. You can't get married in the spring."

Mam turned to stir the scrambled eggs, the subject closed, swept away by her refusal. She calmly continued her work of getting breakfast on the table for her family as Mandy glanced at Lizzie, raised her eyebrows, and shrugged her shoulders helplessly.

BIG DECISIONS

Breakfast Casserole

Makes 6-8 servings

Prep Time: 45 minutes • *Chilling Time: 2-3 hours*
Baking Time: 45 minutes • *Standing Time: 10 minutes*

6-8 medium potatoes,
peeled *or* unpeeled

8 eggs

2 tsp. water

¾ tsp. salt

¼ tsp. pepper

3 cups sharp cheese,
grated

1. Cook potatoes until medium-soft. They should still be slightly crunchy. Cool to room temperature.

2. Refrigerate for 2 hours to make shredding easier.

3. After chilling, shred potatoes and place in the bottom of a greased 9" × 13" baking dish.

4. In separate bowl, beat eggs, water, salt, and pepper together.

5. Pour egg mixture over potatoes and sprinkle with cheese.

6. Bake at 350° for 30 minutes, covered. Take off cover and continue baking for 15 minutes.

7. Let stand 10 minutes before serving.

VARIATIONS:

1. Add more vegetables by adding green peppers or onion to the egg mixture in Step 4.

2. Sprinkle cooked ham, bacon, or sausage over mixture before adding cheese in Step 5.

> *They were saved! No furniture was ruined. All would be well, and Lizzie's joy knew no bounds.*
>
> *"Oh, Stephen, I'm so glad it quit raining. Everything is drying out!" she trilled.*
>
> *She made eggs and toast, heating the canned sausage Mam had given them with the remainder of their canned goods. She would have liked to make pancakes, but she didn't know how, and besides, she had no pancake syrup. She would have to remember to buy some when she went to town with Mam.*
>
> BIG DECISIONS

Creamed Dried Beef

Makes 4-6 servings
Prep Time: 10 minutes • Cooking Time: 20 minutes

2 tsp. butter
¼ lb. chipped dried beef
¼ cup flour
3 cups milk
1 tsp. chopped onion
½ tsp. Worcestershire sauce, *optional*

1. Melt butter in a deep skillet.

2. Stir in chipped beef and cook for 5 minutes.

3. Sprinkle flour over beef and stir to coat evenly.

4. Stirring constantly, slowly pour in milk.

5. Add onion and Worcestershire sauce if you wish.

6. Cook over medium heat until thickened.

7. Serve chipped beef over biscuits, toast, stewed crackers or fried mush. (See recipes for stewed crackers on page 60, and for cornmeal mush on page 58.)

(See recipes for stewed crackers on page 60, and for cornmeal mush on page 58.)

TIP:

Add more flour to thicken creamed dried beef in Step 3 if you wish.

> *Lizzie thought she would suddenly burst apart if someone didn't mention her broad smile. She smiled with all her teeth showing, fairly dancing between the stove and the breakfast table. Mam was preoccupied and didn't say anything more. Lizzie cleared her throat, intending to tell Mam about her upcoming date with Stephen if she didn't notice soon.*
>
> WHEN STRAWBERRIES BLOOM

Sausage Gravy

Makes 8-10 servings

Prep Time: 2 minutes • Cooking Time: 20-25 minutes

½ stick (4 Tbsp.)
butter

2 pounds bulk
sausage

1¼ cups flour

½ tsp. salt

¼ tsp. pepper

2 quarts milk

1. Melt butter in large saucepan.

2. Brown sausage in butter, stirring to break up clumps and cooking until pink is gone.

3. Add flour, salt, and pepper slowly by sprinkling over sausage and stirring constantly.

4. Still stirring, slowly add milk.

5. Mixture will thicken. If mixture gets thicker than you'd like, add more milk.

6. Serve over biscuits, toast, or with stewed crackers (see recipe on page 60).

While Mary did the laundry in the basement, Annie made coffee and put away the things she had brought, including shoofly pie and some of the fresh sausage from the hogs they had just butchered. Lizzie felt very cozy, knowing that having a baby was a special event, especially since Laura was Annie's oldest son Stephen's baby.

BIG DECISIONS

Tomato Gravy

Makes 4-6 servings
Prep Time: 3 minutes • Cooking Time: 10 minutes

1 cup tomato juice
5 Tbsp. flour
¼ tsp. salt
dash of pepper
2 cups milk

1. Pour tomato juice into medium saucepan and bring to a boil.

2. In separate bowl, combine flour, salt, pepper, and milk to form a smooth paste.

3. Pour flour mixture into hot tomato juice, stirring constantly.

4. Heat until thickened.

5. Serve tomato gravy over mush (recipe on page 58), stewed crackers (recipe on page 60), fried potatoes, or eggs and toast.

Oatmeal Pancakes

Makes 8-10 pancakes
Prep Time: 5 minutes • Cooking Time: 2-5 minutes

1 cup dry quick oatmeal

1 cup whole wheat flour

2 eggs

½ cup sour cream

½-¾ cup milk,
until batter is the
consistency you like

1 tsp. baking soda

1 tsp. vinegar

1. In medium bowl, combine dry oatmeal and flour.

2. Stir in eggs, sour cream, and milk.

3. In separate bowl, dissolve soda in vinegar.

4. Stir soda mixture into batter.

5. Spoon batter onto hot skillet.

6. Fry pancakes until golden brown on both sides.

TIP:

Thin batter will make thin pancakes. Thicker batter will make thicker pancakes.

Mam's spatula clattered to the floor as she whirled around, her eyes wide. Emma was laughing with tears in her eyes.

"Really, Emma? For real?" Mam quavered.

"Yes, for real, Mam."

Mam returned to her pancake turning, but Lizzie knew she only went back to her duty to hide her emotions.

WHEN STRAWBERRIES BLOOM

Blueberry Pancakes

Makes 8-10 pancakes
Prep Time: 10 minutes
Cooking Time: 2-5 minutes per skillet- or griddle-full

1½ cups flour

2 Tbsp. sugar

3 tsp. baking powder

1 tsp. salt

1 egg, beaten

1¼ cups milk

3 Tbsp. butter, melted

½-1 cup blueberries, fresh *or* frozen

1. Sift flour, sugar, baking powder, and salt into medium bowl.

2. In separate bowl, combine beaten egg and milk.

3. Add milk mixture and butter to sifted ingredients.

4. Stir just until batter is moistened. Batter will be lumpy.

5. Add blueberries and stir gently to combine.

6. Cook pancakes over high heat until golden brown on both sides.

*And sure enough, the next
Monday morning, the first in May,
Emma fairly danced down the steps,
her cheeks flushed as she whistled
nervously under her breath.*

*Uh-oh, here it comes, Lizzie
thought from her seat on the bench
where she sagged wearily after a late
evening at a singing.*

*Mam had her back turned, flipping
pancakes on the griddle.*

*"Is that you, Emma? Come put the
toast in the broiler," she said.*

WHEN STRAWBERRIES BLOOM

Favorite Pancakes

Makes 10 pancakes

Prep Time: 10 minutes • *Cooking Time: 5 minutes for each pan-full*

1¼ cups all-purpose flour
3 tsp. baking powder
1 Tbsp. sugar
½ tsp. salt
1 cup plus 3 Tbsp. milk
1 egg, beaten
2 Tbsp. vegetable oil
butter

1. Sift flour, baking powder, sugar, and salt into a medium bowl.

2. Add milk, beaten egg, and vegetable oil. Stir just until only small lumps remain.

3. Melt butter in large frying pan or on griddle.

4. Pour batter into pan and cook over high heat.

5. When batter bubbles, flip pancakes.

6. Cook pancakes on second side for approximately 2 minutes.

> *One morning when Emma came down the stairs, her cheeks were flushed with excitement. She looked as if she could absolutely walk on air. In fact, her feet hardly seemed to touch the floor.*
>
> *"Good morning, Emma!" Mam said, turning to add another egg to the pancake mixture.*
>
> *"Morning!"*
>
> RUNNING AROUND
> (AND SUCH)

Baked French Toast

Makes 6-8 servings
Prep Time: 15 minutes
Chilling Time: 8 hours, or overnight • *Baking Time: 35-45 minutes*

⅓ stick (5⅓ Tbsp.) butter
⅓ cup brown sugar
cinnamon to taste
6 slices bread
6 eggs
1 cup milk

1. Melt butter and pour into bottom of 9" × 13" baking pan.

2. Sprinkle brown sugar and cinnamon on top of butter.

3. Layer bread slices on top of sugar and cinnamon.

4. In separate bowl, beat eggs.

5. Add milk and beat well.

6. Pour over bread slices.

7. Refrigerate for 8 hours, or overnight.

8. Bake at 350° for 35-45 minutes, or until browned.

> *It was Saturday morning, when breakfast was always later and much more relaxed than on weekdays, because no one had to hurry off to their jobs or to school. Dat and Mam were contentedly sipping their steaming mugs of morning coffee as they laughed at the twins.*
>
> WHEN
> STRAWBERRIES
> BLOOM

French Toast

Makes 4 servings
Prep Time: 5 minutes • *Cooking Time: 10-15 minutes*

1 egg
⅓ cup milk
½ tsp. cinnamon
4 slices homemade bread
2-4 Tbsp. melted butter
syrup

1. With an egg beater, beat egg, milk, and cinnamon.

2. Pour mixture into a shallow bowl.

3. Dip bread into egg mixture, one slice at a time, being sure to soak both sides.

4. Fry in melted butter until golden brown on each side.

5. Serve with syrup.

> *Lizzie beamed at Mam, basking in her words of praise and acceptance. This all felt so very right and good, so she just continued smiling and laughing as she helped Mam with breakfast, chattering happily with Mandy about their upcoming weekend.*
>
> WHEN STRAWBERRIES BLOOM

Toast for a Group

Makes 8-10 servings
Prep Time: 15 minutes • *Broiling Time: 3-4 minutes*

1 loaf homemade bread

butter

1. Slice bread in thick slices.

2. Lay on baking sheet in single layer.

3. Toast bread under broiler until golden.

4. Turn bread over and toast other side.

5. Slather with butter.

6. Serve.

> *Tall glasses of ice-cold orange juice and crispy toast that was saturated with butter made their meal extra-special.*
>
> *Mam was smiling and saying they had the best coffee she ever tasted. Dat was smiling at Mam as they all enjoyed the delicious food.*
>
> RUNNING AROUND (AND SUCH)

Baked Oatmeal

Makes 6 servings
Prep Time: 10 minutes • Baking Time: 30 minutes

1 stick (8 Tbsp.)
butter, melted

1 cup brown sugar

2 eggs, beaten

3 cups dry quick oatmeal

1 cup milk

2 tsp. baking powder

1 tsp. salt

1. Combine melted butter, brown sugar, and eggs.

2. Stir in remaining ingredients and mix well.

3. Pour into well-greased 8" × 8" casserole or baking dish.

4. Bake at 350° for 30 minutes.

5. Serve, hot, cold, or at room temperature with milk.

> *The breakfast table that morning was absolute bedlam. Everyone congratulating Emma, everyone asking about the wedding plans, everyone talking at once while no one listened.*
>
> WHEN STRAWBERRIES BLOOM

Sturdy Oatmeal

Makes 2 servings
Prep Time: 2-3 minutes
Cooking Time: 5 minutes • Standing Time: 10 minutes

1 cup water

pinch of salt

½ cup dry
quick oats

milk

sugar

1. In medium saucepan, combine water and salt. Bring to a boil.

2. Pour oatmeal into boiling water. Continue boiling until all the oatmeal is covered with bubbles.

3. Turn off heat and let stand 10 minutes.

4. Add milk and sugar before serving.

"Oh, he fixes a dish of oatmeal like ordinary people with sugar and milk, then he plops a piece of chocolate cake in the middle, stirs it up, and eats the whole mess," Emma said.

"Now that is definitely different," John said.

"You want to taste it? I've been eating it for years. It's so good it's habit-forming, like coffee. Tell you what, I'll make you some."

With that, Joshua got up and opened a drawer, selected a small saucepan, filled it with water, and settled it on the stove.

BIG DECISIONS

Creamy Oatmeal

Makes 4 servings

Prep Time: 5-10 minutes • *Standing Time: 30 minutes*

4 cups milk

2 cups dry oats, rolled *or* quick

½ tsp. salt

1. Pour 2" of water into bottom half of a double boiler. Bring water to a boil.

2. In separate bowl, mix milk, oats, and salt together.

3. Pour mixture into top part of double boiler.

4. Turn burner off and let oats stand for 30 minutes, stirring one or two times.

5. Serve.

TIP:

If you don't have a double boiler, simply place a stainless steel bowl on top of a saucepan so that the bowl is suspended over the water and not touching it.

VARIATION:

Oatmeal is delicious served with a piece of chocolate cake!

John and Mandy came up the hill with their black horse, the twins sound asleep in their little car seats in the back seat of the buggy. Mandy had made cookies for their coffee break, and Mam soon had the coffee ready, bringing it up the hill from the farmhouse below.

Lizzie would never forget this whole day. Everything was taken care of, down to the last detail. The curtains were all hung, the bathroom fixtures were in place, and even the canister set Mandy had given her was lined up on the counter top and filled with flour, sugar, oatmeal, and tea.

BIG DECISIONS

Cornmeal Mush

Makes 4 servings

Prep Time: 5 minutes • *Chilling Time: 4-6 hours, or overnight*

3 cups water
1 cup cornmeal
1 tsp. salt
oil for frying

1. Stir together water, cornmeal, and salt in saucepan. Over medium heat, continue stirring until mixture comes to a boil.

2. Turn heat to low and simmer for 20 minutes.

3. Pour into loaf pan and chill 4-6 hours, or overnight.

4. When chilled, cut into ¼"-thick slices

5. Fry in oil until golden brown and crispy. Flip to brown both sides.

VARIATION:

Mush is delicious with fried eggs and ketchup.

Joshua could go on and on about the merits of living with Emma. He didn't try to hide the fact that she was one of the best things that had ever happened to him, and the time he spent on the farm with his wife were the best days of his life. Emma beamed and smiled, naturally basking in the warm words of praise from her husband.

"Surely, though, there are some things that you would change. Surely you're not always blissfully happy every day," Lizzie broke in, always the pessimist.

Joshua shrugged. "I wouldn't know what!"

"Me neither," Emma said softly.

"Come on. Not one thing?" Lizzie asked.

"Oh, maybe little things like not frying the cornmeal mush exactly as crispy as I like it," Joshua laughed.

"Or watching you eat chocolate cake in your oatmeal," Emma said, smiling.

BIG DECISIONS

Stewed Crackers

Makes 4-5 servings

Prep Time: 3 minutes • *Standing Time: 5 minutes*

1 sleeve saltine crackers

2 cups milk

1. Place crackers in medium bowl.

2. Heat milk until almost boiling.

3. Pour heated milk over crackers.

4. Cover for 5 minutes, checking to make sure crackers are submerged in milk.

5. Stir and serve.

TIP:

Add more crackers or more milk to get the consistency you prefer.

Chicken

Dishes

Crispy Baked Chicken

Makes 6-8 servings
Prep Time: 20 minutes • Baking Time: 1-1½ hours

¾ cup cornflakes

1½ tsp. salt

¼ tsp. pepper

1 egg, beaten

3 pounds chicken legs and thighs

1 stick (8 Tbsp.) butter

1. Crush cornflakes to make crumbs in shallow bowl.

2. Add salt and pepper.

3. Beat egg in separate shallow bowl.

4. Line roaster, or 9" × 13" baking pan, with aluminum foil.

5. Dip chicken in egg, and then cornflake mixture.

6. Place in pan lined with aluminum foil.

7. Melt butter and drizzle over chicken.

8. Bake uncovered at 350° for 1-1½ hours, or until juice runs clear when chicken is pricked with a fork.

They also had a frolic on
a Saturday in June, when
they invited all of their
relatives and friends to work
on the addition to the house.
Mam cooked and baked
the week before, preparing
huge amounts of food to feed
the hungry workers. She
made two roasters of fried
chicken and filling. Emma
was always proud of Mam's
culinary skills and worked
diligently to learn all of
Mam's cooking and baking
secrets. Lizzie didn't care.
She just ate the food.

WHEN STRAWBERRIES
BLOOM

Fried Chicken

Makes 5 servings
Prep Time: 20 minutes • Baking Time: 1-1½ hours

1 cup flour

2 tsp. salt

½ tsp. pepper

3 lbs. chicken
legs and thighs

½ stick (4 Tbsp.)
butter

1. Place flour, salt, and pepper
   in shallow bowl or pan.
   Mix together well.

2. Dip each piece of chicken in
   seasoned flour until well coated.

3. In large skillet, melt butter.

4. Carefully place floured chicken
   in melted butter. Fry chicken
   in batches rather than crowd
   chicken. If the skillet is too full,
   the chicken will steam and not
   brown.

5. Fry until golden brown on both
   sides.

6. Line cake pan or jelly-roll pan
   with aluminum foil.

7. Transfer browned chicken to pan.

8. Bake uncovered at 350° for
   1-1½ hours or until tender.

Roasting a Chicken

Makes 6-8 servings
Prep Time: 15 minutes
Roasting Time: about 20 minutes per pound, plus 10-20 minutes extra

1 small to medium
roasting chicken

butter, at room
temperature

salt

½ cup water

1. Rinse chicken and pat dry.

2. Using hands, rub butter on chicken – inside and out.

3. Sprinkle salt liberally on outside.

4. Place chicken in small roaster or pan of your choice.

5. Add water.

6. Bake uncovered at 425° for 20 minutes, and then reduce heat to 375° for remaining time.

TIP:

Calculate about 20 minutes per pound, plus 10-20 minutes more. A good thermometer should register 165° in the center of the chicken when the chicken is fully cooked.

> *Relatives began to arrive very early that morning. The* risht leid, *or the four couples who made the chicken and filling, arrived first. There was lots of work involved in that process, and they had to start early to get the roasting chickens in the oven.*
>
> WHEN
> STRAWBERRIES
> BLOOM

Chicken Stew

Makes 6-8 servings
Prep Time: 30 minutes • Cooking Time: 45 minutes

3 cups cooked chunks
of chicken

1 qt. chicken broth

2 tsp. granular chicken
bouillon

2 cups cubed potatoes

2 cups peas

2 Tbsp. chopped onion

2 cups sliced carrots

1 Tbsp. parsley

1 tsp. salt

pepper to taste

Paste:

3 Tbsp. flour

1 cup water

1. Place first 10 ingredients in an 8-quart kettle.

2. Cover and bring to a boil.

3. Reduce heat and simmer until vegetables are soft.

4. To thicken stew, combine flour and water in separate bowl to make a paste. Stir until smooth.

5. Stir paste into stew to thicken. Continue stirring over low heat until smooth and thickened.

TIP:

This stew is delicious served with dumplings on top (see Dumpling recipe on page 68).

That night at dinner, Mam was busy filling everyone's plate with steaming chicken stew. Large chunks of chicken, white cubes of soft potatoes, orange carrots, peas, and slivers of onion and celery floated in a thick, creamy sauce. Specks of black pepper and little pieces of dark green parsley dotted the broth. Best of all, Lizzie thought, were the mounds of fluffy white dumplings on top. Mam plopped half of one on each plate, and then spooned gravy over it.

WHEN STRAWBERRIES
BLOOM

Dumplings to go with Chicken Stew

Makes 4-6 servings
Prep Time: 10 minutes • Cooking Time: 20 minutes

1½ cups sifted flour
3 tsp. baking powder
¼ tsp. salt
1 egg
½ cup milk

1. In medium bowl, combine flour, baking powder, and salt.

2. Add egg and stir until crumbly.

3. Slowly add milk until dough is sticky. Use only enough milk to moisten ingredients.

4. Drop dumpling batter by tablespoonfuls into simmering stew (after Step 5 in Chicken Stew recipe on page 66).

5. Cook 10 minutes uncovered.

6. Cover. Cook 10 more minutes.

Potpie Noodles to go with Chicken Stew

Makes 6-8 servings

Prep Time: 45 minutes • Cooking Time: 20 minutes

2 cups flour

2 eggs

2-3 Tbsp. milk, *or* cream

chicken broth

> *Mommy Glick had made chicken potpie with large chunks of potatoes swimming in thick chicken gravy. Chunks of white chicken meat were mixed with the potpie squares and sprinkled with bright green parsley. Mommy Glick made her own noodles, too. She mixed egg yolks with flour, and the potpie turned out thick and yellow and chewy. It was the best thing ever to eat with creamy chicken gravy.*
>
> RUNNING AROUND
> (AND SUCH)

1. Put flour in small bowl.

2. Add eggs and stir with fork until crumbly.

3. Add milk to make a soft dough.

4. Sprinkle additional flour on work area.

5. Place dough on floured surface and roll out as thin as possible.

6. Cut into 1" or 2" squares.

7. Drop into Chicken Stew's boiling broth. (See recipe for Chicken Stew on page 66.)

8. Cook for 20 minutes, or until noodles are tender.

Chicken Pie

Makes 4 pies

Prep Time: 30 minutes • *Baking Time: 35-45 minutes*

3 Tbsp. butter

4 ribs celery, chopped

4 medium carrots, chopped

1 large onion, chopped

¼ cup flour

1 tsp. salt

1 cup milk

1 cup chicken broth

10¾-oz. can cream of mushroom soup

4 cups cooked, cut-up chicken

4 9" unbaked pie crusts, plus dough for 4 top crusts

1. In large skillet, melt butter.

2. Add vegetables and cook until soft.

3. Stir in flour and salt.

4. Slowly add milk and broth, stirring constantly.

5. Cook until sauce thickens.

6. Remove from heat and stir in soup.

7. Stir in chicken.

8. Pour into prepared pie crusts and top with pastry top (see Pie Crust recipe on page 215).

9. Bake at 350° for 35-45 minutes.

Quick and Easy Chicken Pie

Makes 4 servings

Prep Time: 15 minutes • Baking Time: 30 minutes

2 cups cooked
mixed vegetables

1 cup cooked and
diced chicken

10¾-oz. can cream
of chicken soup

1 cup buttermilk
baking mix

½ cup milk

1 egg

1. In medium bowl, combine vegetables, chicken, and soup.

2. Pour mixture into 2-quart greased baking dish or 10" pie plate.

3. In separate bowl, stir together baking mix, milk, and egg.

4. Drop by tablespoonfuls over vegetable-chicken mixture.

5. Bake at 400° for 30 minutes.

Chicken Casserole

Makes 6-8 servings

Prep Time: 30 minutes • Baking Time: 35-45 minutes

2 sticks (16 Tbsp.) butter, *divided*

6 cups soft bread cubes

¼ cup minced onion

1 tsp. celery salt

½ tsp. salt

¼ cup flour

½ cup milk

1 cup chicken broth

3 cups cooked and chopped chicken

2 cups cooked peas, *or* green beans

1. Melt 1 stick butter.

2. In large bowl, combine melted butter, bread cubes, onion, celery salt, and salt.

3. Pour into greased 9" × 13" baking dish and bake at 375° for 15 minutes.

4. Meanwhile, in large saucepan, melt other stick of butter.

5. Stir in flour.

6. Stirring constantly over medium heat, add milk and broth.

7. Continuing to stir, cook until thickened.

8. Stir in chicken and peas.

9. Pour mixture over bread cubes and continue baking for 20-30 minutes.

Lizzie was hungry, but it didn't look as if anyone was preparing any food. There wasn't even any coffee or tea on the stove or cookies for a midmorning snack. She couldn't remember anyone talking about lunch.

"Aren't we having coffee break?" Lizzie asked Mam.

"No, we got started a bit late, so we'll just have an early lunch," Mam answered.

WHEN STRAWBERRIES
BLOOM

Chicken Noodle Bake

Makes 6-8 servings
Prep Time: 30 minutes • *Baking Time: 30 minutes*

8-oz. pkg. medium noodles
half a stick (4 Tbsp.) butter
3 Tbsp. flour
2 cups milk
¼ cup chopped onion
1 tsp. salt
⅛ tsp. pepper
2½ cups shredded cheese
2 cups cooked and chopped chicken

1. Cook noodles according to directions on package. Drain noodles.

2. In a separate saucepan, melt butter.

3. Add flour and cook for 2 minutes, stirring constantly. Do not brown.

4. Continue to stir and slowly pour in milk.

5. Add onions, salt, and pepper and cook over medium heat until thickened, stirring continually.

6. Remove from heat and stir in cheese.

7. Mix cheese sauce, noodles, and chicken together in a large bowl.

8. Pour into greased 9" × 13" baking dish and bake at 350° for 30 minutes.

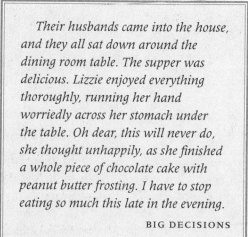

Their husbands came into the house, and they all sat down around the dining room table. The supper was delicious. Lizzie enjoyed everything thoroughly, running her hand worriedly across her stomach under the table. Oh dear, this will never do, she thought unhappily, as she finished a whole piece of chocolate cake with peanut butter frosting. I have to stop eating so much this late in the evening.

BIG DECISIONS

Chicken Gumbo

Makes 10-12 servings

Prep Time: 30 minutes • Baking Time: 30-45 minutes

9 slices bread, toasted and cubed

4 cups cooked and cubed chicken

half a stick (4 Tbsp.) butter, melted

½ cup Miracle Whip salad dressing

4 eggs, beaten

1 cup chicken broth

1 cup milk

1 tsp. salt

2 10¾-oz. cans cream of celery soup

9 slices cheese of your choice

1. Place bread cubes on bottom of greased 9 x 13 baking dish.

2. Sprinkle chicken over top.

3. In separate bowl, combine melted butter, Miracle Whip, eggs, broth, milk, salt, and soup.

4. Pour mixture over chicken.

5. Top with cheese.

6. Bake at 350° for 30-45 minutes, or until lightly browned.

The rest of the day Lizzie housecleaned, ironed curtains, and did any job Mary assigned to her. By the end of the day, she was bone-tired and wished she could go home. She missed Mandy and Mam and Dat, their supper table in the old kitchen, and Jason talking with his mouth full. Everything about home seemed so dear and precious. A wave of homesickness enveloped Lizzie in a gray mist.

RUNNING AROUND (AND SUCH)

Chicken or Beef Gravy

Makes 4 servings
Prep Time: 5 minutes • Cooking Time: 15 minutes

1 pint broth with meat drippings if available

2-3 Tbsp. flour

¼ tsp. salt

dash of pepper

1 cup water

1. Heat broth until boiling.

2. In separate bowl, mix flour, salt, and pepper together. Stir in water to make a smooth paste.

3. Add to broth and stir.

4. Heat until thickened, stirring continually.

5. Stir in the cooked chicken or beef. Serve over mashed potatoes, noodles, rice, or toast points.

TIP:

You can add as much or as little flour-water paste to the broth to make it as thick or thin as you like.

> *After they had bowed their heads in silent prayer, they passed dishes of hot, steaming food—fluffy mashed potatoes, thick beef gravy, and succulent young peas in a cream sauce. Applesauce and small red peppers stuffed with cabbage, crisp green pickles, and lots of bread, butter, and jelly completed the meal.*
>
> RUNNING AROUND (AND SUCH)

Roasht or Chicken Filling

Makes 15 servings

Prep Time: 45 minutes • Baking Time: 1½-2 hours

1 stick (8 Tbsp.) butter

2 cups chopped celery

2 loaves bread, cubed

3 cups cooked and diced chicken

6 eggs, beaten

1 tsp. salt

pepper to taste

1. Melt butter in large skillet.

2. Add celery and sauté until soft.

3. Toss bread and chicken together in a large bowl.

4. Pour celery and eggs over bread mixture.

5. Sprinkle with salt and pepper and mix well.

6. Pour into greased roaster or large baking dish.

7. Bake uncovered at 350° for 1½-2 hours.

8. During baking time, stir occasionally, stirring bread away from sides of pan to prevent burning.

Joshua and Emma and their bridal party cleaned the celery. An Amish wedding had celery in everything, Lizzie claimed, but Emma corrected her, saying only in the roasht and the stewed celery. Oh, yes, and in the afternoon, whole stalks of celery to snack on were placed in tall vases and set on the tables.

WHEN STRAWBERRIES
BLOOM

Ohio Filling

Makes 15 servings

Prep Time: 1 hour • Baking Time: 1½-2 hours

1 cup chopped celery

½ cup diced potatoes

½-1 cup chopped carrots

2 loaves bread, cubed

2 sticks (½ pound) butter, melted

6 eggs, beaten

5-6 cups milk

1 cup chicken broth

1 Tbsp. chicken bouillon

½ tsp. pepper

1 tsp. seasoned salt

2 Tbsp. parley, fresh or dried

2 cups cooked and diced chicken

1. In saucepan, cook celery, potatoes, and carrots over medium heat, in about 1" of water, until tender.

2. In large bowl, toss bread cubes with melted butter.

3. Spread bread cubes onto 2 baking sheets.

4. Toast at 375° in oven for 20 minutes, or until nicely browned.

5. In large mixing bowl, combine eggs, milk, broth, bouillon, pepper, seasoned salt, and parsley.

6. Add chicken, celery, potatoes, carrots, and toasted bread cubes. Mix together gently.

7. Pour into large greased roaster or 1 or 2 baking pans.

8. Bake uncovered at 350° for 1½-2 hours.

9. Stir occasionally.

10. Serve when top is brown and crusty.

> *The best part of Christmas dinner was the Ohio filling. It came out of the oven moist and steaming with a golden brown crust on top. The crust was the best. It tasted like toast with too much butter, Lizzie thought. Mam's version was from her native Holmes County, Ohio, and included potatoes, carrots, and celery chopped into tiny pieces, cubed bread, chicken, and chicken broth. It was so good. There was no other way to describe it except to say it was almost the best thing about Christmas food.*
>
> WHEN STRAWBERRIES BLOOM

Roast Turkey

Prep Time: 20-30 minutes

turkey
butter
salt

Stuffing:
1½ sticks (¾ cup) butter
¾ cup chopped onion
2 large chopped celery ribs
9 cups soft bread cubes
1 tsp. salt
¼ tsp. pepper

TO ROAST TURKEY:

1. Remove giblets from turkey.

2. Stuff turkey if desired.

3. Rub outside of turkey with butter.

4. Sprinkle with salt.

5. Bake at 425° for 20 minutes or until meat thermometer reads 180°. Then reduce heat to 325° for remaining time.

6. For an 8-12 lb. turkey, unstuffed, allow 2¾-3 hours for roasting. For an 8-12 lb. turkey, stuffed, allow 3-3½ hours for roasting.

7. Using a food thermometer, check the internal temperature of the turkey and the stuffing. They should both be 165° at a minimum.

Chicken Dishes

1. In small saucepan, melt butter.

2. Add onions and celery and cook until soft.

3. In separate bowl, combine onions, celery, and bread cubes.

4. Sprinkle with salt and pepper and mix well.

5. Place immediately in cavity of turkey, or bake separately at 375° in a well-greased casserole dish for 20-30 minutes.

> *Sometime Mam roasted a turkey for Christmas, and other years she baked a ham. She would always arrange pineapple rings on the ham and baste it with a bit of the juice while it baked.*
>
> WHEN STRAWBERRIES BLOOM

Turkey Bake

Makes 6-8 servings
Prep Time: 30 minutes • Baking Time: 40 minutes

8 slices bread, cubed, *divided*

2 cups cooked, cubed turkey

2 cups shredded cheese

¼ cup chopped onion

1 Tbsp. butter

2 cups milk

3 eggs

½ tsp. salt

¼ tsp. pepper

1. Place half of bread cubes in well-greased 9" × 9" baking pan or casserole dish.

2. Spread turkey over bread.

3. Sprinkle cheese over turkey.

4. In a small skillet, sauté onion in butter.

5. Spread onion over cheese.

6. Cover with remaining bread cubes.

7. In separate bowl, stir milk, eggs, salt, and pepper together.

8. Pour over casserole.

9. Bake at 350° for 40 minutes.

NOTE:

This casserole is almost a quick version of "roasht" (see page 78).

And so plans were made, with the small group of youth being "officially" started in Cameron County. The girls had great fun cooking supper through trial and error at Leroy Zook's house as the boys did the evening chores. Mary Ann was easy to talk to and, after a few hours together, Lizzie felt as if they had known each other for a long time. Rebecca was also talkative and good-natured with an easy laugh, and her antics never failed to send Lizzie into rounds of helpless laughter.

WHEN STRAWBERRIES BLOOM

Be contented, and do not worry

Or try to catch up with the world's

Uneasiness and speed.

MOTTO FROM AN AMISH
SCHOOL IN PENNSYLVANIA

Meats and Other Main Dishes

Baked Beef Stew

Makes 6-8 servings
Prep Time: 15 minutes • Baking Time: 3 hours

2 pounds cubed
stewing meat

1 cup V-8 juice

6 carrots, sliced

3 medium potatoes,
peeled and cubed

½ cup chopped celery

1 medium onion, sliced

3 Tbsp. minute tapioca

1 slice bread, crumbled

1 cup water

2 Tbsp. brown sugar

1 Tbsp. Worcestershire
sauce

1. In large bowl, combine all ingredients.

2. Mix well.

3. Pour into well-greased 3-quart baking dish.

4. Cover and bake at 325° for 3 hours.

"Rebecca, I'm so glad you're 16. And Mandy and Mary
Ann just turned 16! We're going to have so much fun
together. First of all, the boys are doing chores at Leroy
Zook's place. You know, that old guy that's dating Emma's
friend. They want us to go along and make supper!"

"Does that mean we're going to start having suppers and
singings here now?" Rebecca asked.

"I guess that's up to the parents, but I think everyone
would be glad to have singings, even if the group is small."

WHEN STRAWBERRIES BLOOM

Beef and Potato Loaf

Makes 4-6 servings
Prep Time: 30 minutes • Baking Time: 1½ hours

4 cups raw potatoes

1 Tbsp. chopped onion

1 tsp. salt

For Meat Loaf:

1 pound hamburger

¾ cup milk

½ cup dry oatmeal, quick *or* rolled

¼ cup ketchup

¼ cup diced onion

1 tsp. salt

¼ tsp. pepper

1. Peel potatoes and slice very thin.

2. Place potatoes, onion, and salt into bottom of greased 3-quart casserole dish.

3. Mix together meat loaf ingredients. Shape into loaf.

4. Place meat loaf on top of potatoes.

5. Bake at 350° for 1-1½ hours, or until potatoes are soft.

6. If meat loaf begins to get too dark while baking, cover with foil.

TIP:

Spread additional ketchup over top of meat loaf before baking, if you wish.

Meat Loaf

Makes 8 servings

Prep Time: 30 minutes • Baking Time: 1 hour

For Meat Loaf:

1½ pounds hamburger

¾ cup dry quick oats

1 egg, beaten

¾ cup milk

1½ tsp. salt

¼ cup chopped onion

¼ tsp. pepper

For Sauce:

½ cup ketchup

2 Tbsp. brown sugar

1 Tbsp. prepared mustard

1. Combine meat loaf ingredients in the order given.

2. With clean hands, mix well. Shape into loaf.

3. Place in well-greased pan.

4. Combine sauce ingredients and pour on top.

5. Bake at 350° for 1 hour.

> *"Oh, goody! Then I*
> *can make meat loaf and*
> *barbecue sandwiches*
> *and vegetable soup*
> *and lots of good things*
> *for Stephen's supper,"*
> *Lizzie said, smiling.*
>
> BIG DECISIONS

> *The buttered potatoes,*
> *corn, and meat loaf*
> *tasted good to Lizzie*
> *after a day of traipsing*
> *around in the cold,*
> *trying to keep everyone*
> *happy. She soon forgot*
> *her frustration after all*
> *the youth filed in and*
> *they sat eating the good*
> *food and listening to the*
> *singing.*
> BIG DECISIONS

Hot Roast Hamburger

Makes 6-8 servings
Prep Time: 30 minutes • Baking Time: 1-3 hours

1 pound hamburger
⅔ cup tomato juice
½ cup dry bread crumbs
¼ cup ketchup
1 tsp. salt
2 tsp. Worcestershire sauce
¼ tsp. pepper
6-8 medium potatoes, sliced ½-¾" thick
4-6 medium carrots, sliced
1 large onion, sliced
parsley
salt and pepper to taste

1. In large bowl, combine hamburger, tomato juice, bread crumbs, ketchup, salt, Worcestershire sauce, and pepper.

2. Mix well.

3. Shape into loaf.

4. Place into a large, greased casserole dish or roaster.

5. Add potatoes, carrots, and onions in layers around meat loaf.

6. Sprinkle with parsley, salt, and pepper.

7. Bake at 300° for 2-3 hours, or at 375° for 1-1½ hours.

She tried to savor every moment here on the leaf-strewn, wooded hillside, chattering as only young women can. This was almost their last time together at the youth's supper, and it all took on a surreal quality as Lizzie listened to Sally and Rebecca, smiling to herself as she tore a brittle leaf into many pieces.

It was a bit sad to think that there would be no more weekends of running around with her friends. Not really sad, just nostalgic maybe, kind of wishing you could go back and be 16 all over again. Would there ever be another time in her life quite as exciting as going to Allen County with Emma that very first weekend just after Lizzie turned 16?

BIG DECISIONS

Hamburger Casserole

Makes 8-10 servings
Prep Time: 45-60 minutes • Baking Time: 30-35 minutes

2 pounds hamburger

1 small onion, chopped

3 tsp. salt, *divided*

2 10¾-oz. cans tomato soup

1½ quarts home-canned, *or* 3 15½-oz. cans, green beans

9 medium potatoes

1 egg

¼ tsp. pepper

½ cup warm milk

half a stick (4 Tbsp.) butter, *optional*

1. Brown hamburger, onion, and 2 tsp. salt in skillet until cooked and crumbly.

2. Drain off drippings.

3. In large bowl, combine hamburger, tomato soup, and green beans.

4. Pour into greased 9" × 13" baking dish.

5. Peel, cook, and mash potatoes.

6. When potatoes are mashed, add egg, 1 tsp. salt, pepper, milk, and butter if you wish.

7. Spread potatoes over hamburger mixture.

8. Bake at 350° for 30-35 minutes.

> *"Lizzie, you better start
> thinking about a husband.
> Four more days and it's
> your very first weekend to
> go with me to Allen County.
> Ephraim Yoders are having
> the supper for all the youth.
> Imagine that! Everything
> is planned already! I'm so
> excited to be able to take my
> younger sister along."*
>
> *Lizzie smiled at Emma
> appreciatively. "Do you
> really feel that way?"*
>
> *"Why, of course, Lizzie."*
>
> RUNNING AROUND
> (AND SUCH)

Hamburger Gravy

Makes 8-10 servings
Prep Time: 20 minutes • Cooking Time: 20 minutes

2 pounds hamburger

2 small onions, chopped

1 tsp. salt

¼ tsp. pepper

½ cup flour

3 cups milk

10¾-oz. cream of mushroom soup, *optional*

12-oz. can evaporated milk, *optional*

1. In large skillet, brown hamburger, onion, salt, and pepper.

2. Cook, stirring frequently until no pink remains and meat is crumbly.

3. Stir in flour.

4. Remove from heat and stir in milk.

5. Return to medium heat.

6. Add soup and evaporated milk.

7. Cook, stirring frequently until smooth and thickened.

8. Serve over mashed potatoes.

"Lizzie, you just don't get it. How can I push a wheelbarrow across the newly seeded lawn? Or drag a water hose across it? Or set up the scaffolding? It simply won't work. Besides, it's too late in the season. The sun will be too hot, and we'd have to water constantly if we seeded now." Picking up his fork, Stephen resumed eating his mashed potatoes and hamburger gravy.

Lizzie didn't say anything and only watched him eat, thinking he had an awfully big mouthful of food and that she didn't like him very much.

BIG DECISIONS

Camper's Special

Makes 6-8 servings
Prep Time: 15 minutes • Cooking Time: 30 minutes

1 pound ground beef

1 medium onion, chopped

16-oz. can pork and beans

¾ cup ketchup

2 tsp. prepared mustard

3 cups cubed and cooked potatoes

salt and pepper to taste

1. In a large skillet, brown ground beef and onion. Drain off drippings.

2. Stir in beans, ketchup, and mustard.

3. Cook until hot and bubbly.

4. Add potatoes and heat through, about 30 minutes.

5. Sprinkle with salt and pepper.

TIP:

To cook potatoes, peel and cube. Place in saucepan along with ¾ cup water. Cover and cook over low to medium heat until potatoes are tender. Stir frequently to prevent sticking. Add water if needed while potatoes cook so that they don't cook dry.

"Does this mean that we have to stay home on weekends and everyone is going to be all serious and sad and I can't go camping this weekend?" she burst out, leaning against the countertop as she searched Mam's face.

Mam smiled a very small smile. "No, of course not. Dat is still alive and well and will continue to be all right for quite some time. Actually, he shouldn't be showing too many signs of the disease for up to a few years, other than his stumbling and blurry vision. So, no, Lizzie, you can go camping, of course. Our family life will just go on much the same as it always has."

WHEN STRAWBERRIES BLOOM

Macaroni and Hamburger Casserole

Makes 6-8 servings
Prep Time: 30 minutes • *Baking Time: 25 minutes*

1½ cups uncooked macaroni

1½ quarts water

2 tsp. salt

¼ stick (2 Tbsp.) butter

¼ cup minced onion

1 lb. hamburger

2 tsp. flour

1 cup chopped green bell pepper

15½-oz. can diced tomatoes, undrained

½-1 cup grated cheese of your choice

1. Cook macaroni in salted water until tender.

2. Drain and set aside.

3. Melt butter in medium skillet.

4. Fry onion and hamburger in butter until hamburger is brown and crumbly.

5. Stir in flour, peppers, and tomatoes.

6. Combine hamburger mixture and macaroni.

7. Pour into greased casserole dish.

8. Sprinkle with cheese.

9. Bake at 350° for 25 minutes.

That evening at supper, Dat had asked Lizzie why she was eating less.

"I'm not hungry," she said.

"You must be sick then," Dat said, taking a big spoonful of macaroni and cheese.

Lizzie swallowed, watching him lift a steaming forkful to his mouth, shaking his head because it burned his tongue. She could eat the whole dish of macaroni all by herself, she was so hungry. For a moment, she felt like crying, but the thought of her weight and the size of her waistline filled her with determination. She would go through with it.

RUNNING AROUND
(AND SUCH)

Pizza Casserole

Makes 8-10 servings
Prep Time: 20 minutes • Baking Time: 35 minutes

1 pound hamburger

¼ cup chopped onion

8-oz. pkg. medium noodles

10¾-oz. can cream of mushroom soup

15-oz. jar pizza sauce

pepperoni, *optional*

chopped green bell peppers, *optional*

2 cups shredded mozzarella cheese

1. Brown hamburger in medium skillet. Stir frequently to break up clumps.

2. Add onions. Continue cooking until tender.

3. In separate pan, cook noodles until soft. Drain.

4. Stir together hamburger and noodles in large mixing bowl.

5. Pour soup and pizza sauce over hamburger mixture and stir to combine.

6. Pour into greased 3-quart baking dish.

7. Top with pepperoni and peppers if you wish.

8. Sprinkle with cheese.

9. Bake at 350° for 35 minutes.

Poor Man's Steak

Makes 4-5 servings
Prep Time: 20 minutes
Chilling Time: 8-10 hours, or overnight • *Baking Time: 45 minutes*

1 pound hamburger

1 cup cracker crumbs, *or* dry oatmeal

1 small onion, chopped

1 tsp. salt

¼ tsp. pepper

1 cup milk

¼ stick (2 Tbsp.) butter

10¾-oz. can cream of mushroom soup

1. In large bowl, mix hamburger, cracker crumbs, onion, salt, pepper, and milk together.

2. Shape into loaf.

3. Refrigerate 8-10 hours, or overnight.

4. Remove from refrigerator and slice into ½"-thick slices.

5. Brown each slice in butter in skillet.

6. Place browned slices in greased 9" × 13" baking pan.

7. Cover with soup.

8. Bake at 350°, covered, for 45 minutes.

VARIATION:

Substitute gravy for cream of mushroom soup, if you wish.

Pour Pizza

Makes 8-10 servings
Prep Time: 20 minutes • Baking Time: 30-35 minutes

1 pound hamburger
1 small onion, chopped
1 tsp. salt
¼ tsp. pepper
1 cup flour
2 eggs
⅔ cup milk
⅛-¼ tsp. dried oregano
1-2 cups shredded cheese

1. In medium skillet, brown hamburger, onion, salt, and pepper together.

2. In separate bowl, combine flour, eggs, milk, and oregano to create a batter.

3. Pour batter into well-greased 7" × 11" baking dish.

4. Top with hamburger mixture.

5. Bake at 350° for 15-20 minutes.

6. Remove from oven and sprinkle with cheese.

7. Return to oven for 15 minutes more.

TIP:

Pour Pizza may be served with warmed spaghetti/pizza sauce for dipping.

Before they went to the big K-Mart store, they stopped for their favorite treat—pizza. That was one thing they never disagreed on. Pizza was their favorite restaurant food. Lizzie knew that pizza and all the big sandwiches, French fries, fried mushrooms, and whatever were terribly high in calories and everything else that was not good for you, but she never cared, figuring a few such meals weren't going to hurt her.

Lizzie liked going to restaurants with Stephen. He always told Lizzie the same thing—that he didn't know how to pronounce the words, so she should order for him. Then he would show her the item he wanted and pronounce it in some outrageous fashion, so that she always laughed when the time came to order.

BIG DECISIONS

Barbecued Ham Slices

Makes 12-16 servings
Prep Time: 20 minutes • Baking Time: 2 hours

1 Tbsp. butter

¼ cup chopped onions

½ cup ketchup

⅓ cup water

2 Tbsp. brown sugar

1 Tbsp. Worcestershire sauce

2 Tbsp. white vinegar

12 slices boneless ham

1. Melt butter in medium saucepan.

2. Add onion and cook until soft.

3. In separate bowl, combine ketchup, water, brown sugar, Worcestershire sauce, and vinegar.

4. Add to saucepan with onions and bring to a boil.

5. Simmer for 5 minutes.

6. Arrange ham slices in a single layer in large greased casserole dish (or dishes) or roaster.

7. Pour sauce over ham.

8. Bake at 350° for 1½ hours. Baste occasionally with sauce.

Supper was delicious, but no one was really hungry. Lizzie pushed the ham and potatoes around on her plate, wishing the wedding would be over now. It was interesting watching John trying not to watch Mandy. Lizzie talked and laughed with him since she saw him almost every weekend, and he was a good friend. Mandy was new to running around, so she was unaccustomed to any of the young men from the youth group, and she sat shy and quiet.

John was quite enamored with Mandy, Lizzie could easily tell. He must have found her pleasant company, too, since by the end of the evening as the singing was winding down, they sat deep in a serious conversation. As far as they were concerned, Lizzie thought, there was no one else at the wedding.

WHEN STRAWBERRIES BLOOM

Old-Fashioned Baked Ham

Makes 10-15 servings
Prep Time: 30 minutes • Baking Time: 70-75 minutes

5-lb. ham

½ cup brown sugar

¼ tsp. ground cloves, *optional*

1 tsp. dry mustard

1 Tbsp. vinegar

8-oz. can pineapple slices, with 2 Tbsp. juice reserved

12-20 maraschino cherries, *optional*

> *Sometime Mam roasted a turkey for Christmas, and other years she baked a ham. She would always arrange pineapple rings on the ham and baste it with a bit of the juice while it baked.*
>
> WHEN STRAWBERRIES BLOOM

1. Bake ham, uncovered, in roaster at 350° for 30 minutes.

2. While ham is baking, combine brown sugar, cloves, mustard, vinegar, and 2 Tbsp. pineapple juice to make glaze.

3. Remove ham from oven and score.

4. Place pineapple, and cherries if you wish, on top of ham.

5. Spoon glaze over fruit and ham.

6. Bake for another 40-45 minutes, basting occasionally.

Ham Loaf

Makes 8-10 servings
Prep Time: 30 minutes • Baking Time: 1½ hours

For Ham Loaf:
1 pound ground ham

1 pound bulk sausage

2 cups soft bread crumbs

2 eggs, beaten

1 cup sour cream

1 tsp. dry mustard

⅛ tsp. paprika

⅛ tsp. black pepper

For Sauce:
½ cup packed brown sugar

½ cup pineapple juice

1 Tbsp. clear-jel, *or* cornstarch

1. In large bowl, mix together all ham loaf ingredients.

2. Form into a loaf and place in greased loaf pan.

3. Bake uncovered at 350° for 1 hour.

4. While ham loaf is baking, prepare sauce.

5. Combine ingredients for sauce in small pan.

6. Bring to a boil. Stir frequently over medium heat until smooth and thickened.

7. When ham loaf has baked for an hour, remove from oven.

8. Drain ham loaf drippings into prepared sauce.

9. Baste ham loaf with sauce.

10. Return to oven and bake 30 more minutes, or until lightly browned.

Green Bean and Sausage Casserole

Makes 6-8 servings
Prep Time: 45 minutes • Baking Time: 30 minutes

1-1½ pounds sausage,
bulk *or* link

1 quart home-canned,
or 2 15½-oz. cans,
green beans

6 medium-sized
potatoes

¾ cup water

¼ pound grated
cheddar cheese

10¾-oz. can cream of
mushroom soup

1. Brown sausage in skillet, stirring frequently to break up clumps until no pink remains.

2. Drain off drippings.

3. Place sausage in large mixing bowl.

4. Drain green beans. Add to mixing bowl with meat.

5. Peel and cut potatoes into cubes.

6. Place cubed potatoes in saucepan with ¾ cup water.

7. Cover. Cook over low to medium heat until tender. Stir frequently to prevent sticking. Add more water if needed so potatoes don't cook dry.

8. When fully cooked, drain and add to meat and green beans in bowl.

9. Stir together well.

10. Pour into greased 9" × 13" baking dish.

11. Add cheese and soup. Stir to combine.

12. Bake at 350° for 30 minutes.

> *While Mary did the laundry in the basement, Annie made coffee and put away the things she had brought, including shoofly pie and some of the fresh sausage from the hogs they had just butchered. Lizzie felt very cozy, knowing that having a baby was a special event, especially since Laura was Annie's oldest son Stephen's baby.*
>
> BIG DECISIONS

Sausage Potato Casserole

Makes 8-10 servings
Prep Time: 30 minutes • Baking Time: 70-80 minutes

1 pound bulk pork sausage, *divided*

10¾-oz. can cream of mushroom soup

¾ cup milk

¼ cup chopped onion

½ tsp. salt

½ tsp. pepper

½ tsp. parsley

3 cups raw potatoes, sliced thinly, *divided*

1 cup shredded cheese

1. In a large skillet, brown sausage. Stir frequently to break up clumps and until no pink remains Drain off drippings.

2. In separate bowl, mix together soup, milk, onion, and seasonings.

3. In a casserole dish, layer half the potatoes, then sausage, then soup mixture.

4. Repeat layers until ingredients are all used.

5. Cover and bake at 350° until potatoes are tender, about 60-70 minutes.

6. Remove from oven and sprinkle with cheese.

7. Return to oven, uncovered, until cheese is melted, about 10 more minutes.

Lizzie threw down her book bag, folding into a kitchen chair with a sigh.

"What does that mean, Mam?" she asked, her fingers plucking nervously at the rip in the plastic tablecloth.

Mam turned from the sink where she was peeling potatoes for the evening meal. Taking up the corner of her apron, she dried her hands on it before sitting down at the table.

Her eyes looked tired. The red veins running through the whites of her eyes were more noticeable when she took off her glasses and wiped them with the dry corner of her apron. Putting her glasses back on her face, she smiled at Lizzie, only to have one corner of her mouth drop immediately as her nostrils flared and tears came of their own accord, despite her best effort to hold them back.

"I don't know, Lizzie, really, I don't," Mam said softly. "We have plenty of literature the doctor gave us to read, so I'm sure till the evening is over we'll know more about MS. I'm especially interested in understanding why Dat doesn't have the full ability to walk like he used to. Same thing with his eyes."

WHEN STRAWBERRIES BLOOM

Homemade Pizza

Makes 6 servings
Prep Time: 10 minutes
Rising Time: 30 minutes • Baking Time: 25-30 minutes

1 cup warm water

1 pkg., *or* 1 Tbsp. dry, active yeast

1 tsp. salt

2 Tbsp. oil

2½-3 cups flour

sauce, cheese, and toppings of your choice

1. Pour warm water into medium-sized bowl.

2. Add yeast and stir.

3. Let stand until bubbly, approximately 2-5 minutes.

4. Stir in salt and oil.

5. Add flour and stir.

6. Let dough rise for 30 minutes.

7. Press dough into well-greased 10"×15"×1" baking pan.

8. Bake dough for 10 minutes at 400°.

9. Remove from oven. Add sauce, cheese, and toppings of your choice.

10. Bake 15-20 minutes more at 400°.

11. Let stand a few minutes before serving.

"It's okay. Sharon's mom made pizza!"

The kitchen had a warm, spicy, tomatoey smell, which mixed well with the aroma of homemade yeast dough. Lizzie's stomach rumbled unexpectedly, reminding her of how hungry she really was. Always watching her weight, she hadn't eaten any lunch or supper, only breakfast and one chocolate chip cookie that afternoon. She always wanted to feel thin, especially on running-around weekends, so often on Saturdays she ate very little.

Sharon's mother, Cathy, was bustling between the table and the oven, setting two huge, round pizzas on the table. She grinned at Lizzie and Mandy.

WHEN STRAWBERRIES BLOOM

Baked Macaroni and Cheese

Makes 6 servings

Prep Time: 30 minutes • *Baking Time: 30 minutes*

1½ cups uncooked macaroni

5 Tbsp. butter, *divided*

3 Tbsp. flour

1½ cups milk

1 cup shredded cheddar cheese

½ cup cubed American cheese

½ tsp. salt

¼ tsp. pepper

2 Tbsp. dried bread crumbs

1. Cook macaroni according to directions on package.

2. Drain and put in greased 2-quart baking dish.

3. In medium saucepan, melt 4 Tbsp. butter.

4. Add flour and stir until smooth.

5. Stirring constantly, slowly pour in milk.

6. Boil for 2 minutes stirring continually.

7. Reduce heat to medium.

8. Stir in cheeses, salt, and pepper.

9. Pour over macaroni and mix well.

10. In separate saucepan, melt remaining butter.

11. Add bread crumbs and brown lightly.

12. Sprinkle bread crumbs over macaroni.

13. Bake uncovered at 350° for 30 minutes.

> *Well, there was half of a small saucepan of macaroni and cheese left. Lizzie got a clean fork from the drawer and ate great comforting mouthfuls of the gooey, cheesy dish. She didn't care if she gained five pounds.*
>
> BIG DECISIONS

Floating Islands

Makes 6-8 servings
Prep Time: 15 minutes • Baking Time: 20-30 minutes

1 pound hot dogs

6 cups mashed potatoes

½-¾ pound cheese, cut in long, narrow strips

sauerkraut, *optional*

1. Heat hot dogs in saucepan until warm in center.

2. Remove from pan and cut a slit down the length of each hot dog.

3. Fill with mashed potatoes.

4. Place cheese on top of potatoes.

5. Place hot dogs on cookie sheet or jelly-roll pan.

6. Bake at 350° for 20-30 minutes, or until well browned.

VARIATION:

Sauerkraut goes well with Floating Islands. Heat the sauerkraut in a separate saucepan.

As the sun slipped behind the mountain, Marvin and Reuben started a roaring campfire while Stephen got out folding chairs. They all started roasting hot dogs and burning marshmallows to a black crisp.

Stephen brought his chair over close to hers and sat down beside her. Lizzie smiled.

"Are you having fun?" he asked quietly and only for her ears to hear.

WHEN STRAWBERRIES BLOOM

Soups and Sandwiches

Chicken Corn Soup

Makes 6 servings
Prep Time: 20 minutes • Cooking Time: 30-45 minutes

½ stick (4 Tbsp.) butter

¾-1 cup chopped celery

¾-1 cup chopped onion

3-4 cups water

1 quart corn

4 cups cooked and diced chicken

6-7 tsp. chicken bouillon

2 Tbsp. parsley flakes

1 Tbsp. salt

½-1 tsp. pepper

4 oz. uncooked noodles, *optional*

1. Melt butter in large saucepan.

2. Cook celery and onion in butter until soft.

3. Add water.

4. Stir in corn, chicken, chicken bouillon, parsley, salt, and pepper. Bring to boil.

5. Add noodles if you wish. Allow to simmer until noodles are tender, about 10 more minutes.

TIP:

Add more water and chicken bouillon if necessary to have the consistency and flavor of soup that you like.

So Lizzie ended up not dressing chickens that day. Emma told her she didn't pity her if she couldn't make good chicken potpie or chicken corn soup after she was married.

"I'm not going to get married, so don't worry about me," Lizzie shot back.

Emma looked at her teasingly. "Didn't look like it Sunday evening!"

RUNNING AROUND
(AND SUCH)

Ham, Green Beans, and Potato Stew

Makes 8 servings

Prep Time: 20 minutes • Cooking Time: 30-45 minutes

4 cups cooked and cubed ham

4 cups cubed raw potatoes

2 quarts ham broth, *or* water

1 quart canned, *or* fresh, green beans

salt and pepper to taste

1. Cook ham, potatoes, and broth in large stockpot until potatoes are soft.

2. Add green beans. Heat through if using canned beans. If using fresh beans, cook until beans are as tender as you like them.

3. Sprinkle with salt and pepper.

4. Stir to combine.

Ham Chowder

½ stick (4 Tbsp.) butter

½ cup minced onions

½ cup chopped celery

1 cup cooked and diced ham

2 cups peeled and diced potatoes

½ cup water

3 Tbsp. flour

1½ tsp. salt

¼ tsp. pepper

5 cups milk

1. Melt butter in large saucepan.

2. Add onions, celery, and ham.

3. Cook until onions and celery are soft.

4. Add potatoes and ½ cup water.

5. Cook 10 minutes, or until potatoes are soft.

6. Stir in flour, salt, and pepper until well blended.

7. Stir in milk until well blended.

8. Let simmer 15 minutes. Stir frequently to make sure the chowder's creamy base is smooth and thickened.

Ham and Bean Soup

Makes 8-10 servings

Prep Time: 15 minutes • Cooking Time: 30-45 minutes

8 cups fully cooked and cubed ham

4 cups diced onions

1 stick (8 Tbsp.) butter

2 quarts water

4 quarts cooked Northern beans, drained

1. In a 12-quart stockpot, cook ham and onions in butter until onions are soft.

2. Add water and beans.

3. Cover. Over medium heat, bring to a boil. Allow to simmer 30 minutes.

4. Stir from time to time. If soup thickens beyond what you like, add more water, 1-2 cups at a time.

One afternoon, when the leaves were turning colors and the breeze was a bit chilly, Lizzie and Dora sat by the oak tree with their sweaters wrapped around them as they finished their lunches. Lizzie leaned back against the rough bark of the oak tree and closed her eyes, sighing.

RUNNING AROUND (AND SUCH)

Cheeseburger Soup

Makes 8 servings
Prep Time: 20 minutes • Cooking Time: 45-50 minutes

½ pound ground beef

¾ cup chopped onions

¾ cup shredded carrots

¾ cup chopped celery

½ stick (4 Tbsp.) butter, cut into pieces

1 tsp. parsley

3 cups chicken broth

3 cups peeled and diced potatoes

¼ cup flour

2 cups cubed Velveeta cheese

1¾ cups milk

½ tsp. salt

¼ tsp. pepper

½ tsp. celery salt

1. In large saucepan, brown ground beef. Stir frequently to break up clumps.

2. Add onions, carrots, celery, butter, and parsley. Cook until vegetables are soft.

3. In a separate bowl, combine remaining ingredients.

4. Pour over beef mixture.

5. Heat until boiling.

6. Reduce heat and simmer, covered, about 30-40 minutes, or until potatoes are soft.

> *Mandy and Emma were already doing the dishes, and when Lizzie finished eating, they started deciding whose job it was to do the Saturday cleaning, who would do laundry, and who would tackle the lawn-mowing.*
>
> WHEN STRAWBERRIES BLOOM

Beef Vegetable Soup

Makes 12 servings

Prep Time: 20-30 minutes • Cooking Time: 2-3¼ hours

2 pounds cubed stewing meat, cut into bite-sized pieces

1 quart tomato juice

⅓ cup chopped onion

1 tsp. salt

¼ tsp. chili powder

1 cup chopped celery

1 cup chopped raw carrots

2 cups diced raw potatoes

16-oz. can, *or* frozen pkg., corn

16-oz. can, *or* frozen pkg., green beans

8 cups water

16-oz. can, *or* frozen pkg., peas

1. In large saucepan, combine meat, tomato juice, onion, salt, and chili powder.

2. Cover and cook over medium-low heat for 1-2 hours, or just until meat is tender.

3. Skim off any fat that has surfaced.

4. Stir in all vegetables, except peas. Add water.

5. Cover and simmer 45-60 minutes, or until vegetables are soft.

6. Stir in peas and cook another 10-15 minutes, or until the peas are heated through.

TIPS:

1. When making vegetable soup, use whatever vegetables you prefer or have on hand.

2. You can also use fresh, instead of canned or frozen, vegetables.

> They talked most of the way home, and, as usual, Lizzie could hardly wait to get there because she was bursting with lots of things to tell Mam. Emma and Mandy were away working, she knew, but it was lunch-time, so Dat would be in the house.
> "How did it go, Lizzie?" he asked, as she hurried in the door.
> "Oh, good! Really good. Except a little, first-grade girl almost cried, and Dat, I mean it, they're so loud after I dismiss them, it isn't even normal. They yell good-bye with all their might."
> Dat chuckled as he took a bite of homemade vegetable soup.
>
> WHEN STRAWBERRIES BLOOM

Hamburger Veggie Soup

Makes 15-20 servings

Prep Time: 30 minutes • Cooking Time: 30-45 minutes

2½ quarts tomato juice

2 quarts cooked beans of your choice, drained, *or* 4 15½-oz. cans of beans of your choice, drained

2 cups chopped celery

2 cups sliced carrots

1 quart corn, *or* 2 1-lb. pkgs. frozen corn

4 cups peeled and cubed raw potatoes

1½ pounds hamburger

2 large bell peppers, chopped

2 large onions, chopped

2 Tbsp. minced parsley

1. In large stockpot, mix together tomato juice, beans, celery, carrots, corn, and potatoes.

2. In skillet, cook hamburger, peppers, and onions together. Stir frequently to break up clumps of meat.

3. Drain hamburger and stir into soup.

4. Bring to a boil, then reduce heat and simmer until vegetables are as soft as you like them.

5. Top each bowl of soup with minced parsley.

"How did it feel to have Lizzie for a teacher?" Mam asked.

Jason's mouth was stuffed with pickles, so he nodded his head before bending it to eat the other half of his sandwich in one bite.

Dat shook his head, watching Jason eat.

"As soon as you have time, you can answer Mam," he said, his eyes twinkling.

Jason swallowed and nodded his head again. "Good. I think she's going to be all right. She's a good teacher!"

He started slurping soup, so Lizzie knew that was as much as he would say. She looked at Mam, beaming, and Mam smiled back.

"Good for you, Lizzie. I knew you could do it. Do you think you'll like it? This is only the first day, you know."

WHEN STRAWBERRIES BLOOM

Cream of Tuna Soup

Makes 6 servings
Prep Time: 5 minutes • Cooking Time: 15-20 minutes

6-oz. can tuna, in water *or* oil

½ stick (4 Tbsp.) butter

4 Tbsp. flour

1 tsp. salt

½ tsp. pepper

6 cups milk, *divided*

¾ cup shredded cheese of your choice, *optional*

1. If using tuna in water, melt butter in saucepan. Drain tuna and fry lightly in butter.

2. If using tuna in oil, simply fry tuna in the oil. No need to use butter.

3. Stir in flour, salt, and pepper. Blend well.

4. Over medium heat, add 2 cups of milk, stirring constantly.

5. Cook until thickened.

6. Stir in remaining milk until well blended.

7. Heat, continuing to stir frequently, until hot but not boiling.

8. If you wish, stir shredded cheese into soup just before serving.

Chunky Tomato Soup

Makes 6-8 servings
Prep Time: 5 minutes • *Cooking Time: 20-30 minutes*

¼ cup chopped onions

¼ stick (2 Tbsp.) butter

1 quart home-canned, *or* 2 15½-oz. cans, stewed tomatoes, undrained

1 tsp. salt

pepper to taste

¼ tsp. baking soda

2 quarts milk

1. In large stockpot, fry onions in butter until soft.

2. Add tomatoes, salt, pepper, and baking soda. Mix well.

3. Heat until boiling.

4. In separate saucepan, heat milk until almost boiling. Skin will form on top.

5. Remove from heat.

6. Pour hot milk into tomato mixture, stirring constantly.

7. Serve.

Potato Soup

Makes 4-6 servings

Prep Time: 20 minutes • Cooking Time: 20-30 minutes

4 medium uncooked potatoes, peeled and grated

1 medium carrot, peeled and grated

2 Tbsp. diced onions

2½-3 cups water, *divided*

2-3 chicken bouillon cubes

1-2 tsp. parsley

4 cups milk

¼ stick (2 Tbsp.) butter

2 Tbsp. flour

½-1 cup water

1. Place potatoes, carrots, and onions in medium saucepan.

2. Add 2 cups water and chicken bouillon cubes.

3. Cook, covered, over medium-low heat until vegetables are tender. Stir frequently

4. Add parsley, milk, and butter.

5. In separate bowl, combine flour and ½-1 cup water to make a paste. Blend together until smooth.

6. Stir flour paste into hot soup to thicken. Continue stirring over heat until soup broth becomes smooth and thickens.

"We are going to have to sell Teeny and Tiny," Dat said.

"Why?" Emma asked, stopping halfway with a bite of potato soup.

"Because we really need the money, and because it costs too much to feed three ponies. Mam thinks it would be best. I do, too, of course, but I wish we could keep them, I really do," he finished.

RUNNING AROUND
(AND SUCH)

Creamy Tomato Soup

Makes 4 servings

Prep Time: 5 minutes • *Cooking Time: 10-15 minutes*

½ stick (4 Tbsp.) butter
4 Tbsp. flour
½ tsp. salt
4 cups milk
2 cups tomato juice

1. Melt butter in medium-sized saucepan.

2. Stir in flour and salt until mixture is smooth.

3. Over medium heat, and stirring constantly, slowly pour in milk.

4. Cook, stirring continually, until thickened.

5. Slowly stir in tomato juice and heat until warm. Do not boil.

There wasn't much time to think, with getting Mandy settled on the sofa and finding a cool, clean white sheet and pillow for her. John was hungry, and it was getting close to milking time, so Mam hurried around the kitchen, fixing toasted ham and cheese sandwiches and tomato soup while Lizzie unpacked the accumulation of things from the hospital.

BIG DECISIONS

Rivvel Soup

Makes 4 servings
Prep Time: 10 minutes • Cooking Time: 8-10 minutes

1 quart milk
¼ stick (2 Tbsp.) butter
1 cup flour
½ tsp. salt
1 egg, well beaten
salt and pepper to taste

1. In large saucepan, heat milk and butter until boiling.

2. In separate bowl, combine flour, salt, and egg. Mix with hands or table fork until small lumps appear.

3. Break off pieces, each about ½" round, known as "rivvels," and drop one-by-one into boiling milk.

4. Stir frequently to keep rivvels suspended in broth and to prevent them from clumping together.

5. When all rivvels are in soup, reduce heat to low and simmer 5 minutes.

6. Season with salt and pepper to taste.

Soups and Sandwiches

Cold Milk Soup

Makes 1 serving
Prep Time: 5 minutes

1 slice bread
1 cup fruit, fresh *or* canned
1 cup very cold milk
sugar, *optional*

1. Crumble bread into bowl.

2. Pour fruit and milk over bread.

3. Sprinkle with sugar if you wish.

4. Multiply as many times as needed for the number of persons eating.

NOTE:

This fast, usually summertime, soup is refreshing and filling. It's good for snacks and for when the cook is busy in the garden or canning the garden's bounty.

Barbecued Chicken Sandwiches

Makes 2-4 servings

Prep Time: 15 minutes • Cooking Time: 15-20 minutes

2 cups cooked and
diced chicken

1 small onion, chopped

¼ cup brown sugar

1 Tbsp. Worcestershire
sauce

½ cup ketchup

1 Tbsp. prepared
mustard

½ tsp. salt

dash of pepper

1. Chop chicken into small pieces and place in medium saucepan.

2. In separate bowl, combine remaining ingredients.

3. Pour over chicken.

4. Bring to a boil, then reduce heat and allow to simmer 15-20 minutes, or until heated through.

5. Serve hot on sandwich rolls.

She opened the lid of her lunchbox and pulled out her plastic container of juice. She took long gulps of the ice-cold drink. She felt so much better as she unwrapped her sandwich made with Mam's homemade bread, sliced turkey, white American cheese, and lettuce. It was so good, she thought, as she munched it down with a handful of crunchy potato chips. She was so hungry that she didn't worry about counting calories at all. After all, you couldn't work if you didn't eat.

Her spirits lifting, Lizzie watched the leaves swaying in the breeze.

RUNNING AROUND (AND SUCH)

Barbecued Ham Sandwiches

Makes 15-20 servings
Prep Time: 15 minutes
Cooking Time: 30 for stovetop; 1 hour for oven

3 Tbsp. butter

2 pounds chipped,
fully cooked ham

1 Tbsp. flour

3 Tbsp. brown sugar

1 cup ketchup

¼ cup vinegar

1 cup water

1 Tbsp. Worcestershire
sauce

1. Melt butter in large skillet.

2. Add ham. Cook until browned, about 10 minutes, stirring occasionally.

3. Sprinkle flour over ham.

4. In separate bowl, combine remaining ingredients. Pour over ham.

5. Simmer on stovetop 30 minutes, or transfer to greased 2-quart baking dish and bake at 250° for 1 hour.

6. Serve on sandwich rolls.

TIP:

Leftovers freeze well and are easy to reheat later.

> *Once when Lizzie was little and the leaves were orange and red, Dat said to Mam, "Let's hitch up Bess and go to the mountain today."*
>
> *"We could," Mam agreed and smiled at Dat.*
>
> *"Good. After dishes and a Bible story, I'll hitch up the buggy and you can pack a lunch."*
>
> RUNNING AROUND
> (AND SUCH)

Cheeseburgers

Makes 10 servings

Prep Time: 10-15 minutes • Cooking Time: about 10 minutes

2 pounds
hamburger

2 eggs

2 cups soft
bread crumbs

1½ tsp. salt

¾ cup chopped
onion

¼ cup milk

sliced cheese of
your choice

1. Place hamburger in medium bowl.

2. In separate bowl, beat eggs.

3. Add bread crumbs, salt, onion, and milk to eggs.

4. Add mixture to hamburger and mix well.

5. Using clean hands, form mixture into 10 hamburger patties.

6. In large nonstick skillet, brown burgers over medium heat. Do in batches rather than crowd skillet, so burgers can brown.

7. When first side is brown (about 5 minutes), flip. Cook until second side is well-browned, about 10 minutes total for both sides.

8. Slice cheese and place one slice on each burger. Remove from heat.

9. Cheeseburgers are ready when cheese is melted. Serve in sandwich buns.

They finished painting the kitchen without any further incidents. Then Hannah made a special meal of delicious cheeseburgers much later than the usual lunch hour. She served tall glasses of Coke with tinkling ice cubes, and lots of ketchup, mayonnaise, tomatoes, onions, and lettuce to put on their sandwiches.

RUNNING AROUND
(AND SUCH)

Beef Barbecue Sandwiches

Makes 8-10 servings
Prep Time: 15 minutes • Cooking Time: 30 minutes

2 pounds hamburger

1 onion, chopped

½ cup ketchup

2 Tbsp. brown sugar

2 Tbsp. prepared mustard

1 tsp. vinegar, *or* Worcestershire sauce

1 tsp. salt

1. In medium saucepan, fry hamburger and onion until brown and crumbly. Stir frequently to break up clumps of meat.

2. In separate bowl, stir together ketchup, brown sugar, mustard, vinegar, and salt.

3. Pour over hamburger.

4. Stir to combine and heat thoroughly over medium heat, about 15 minutes.

5. Serve on sandwich rolls.

TIP:

Serve with cheese slices, pickles, and more mustard as optional toppings for the sandwiches.

At noon, Darwin turned off the egg-grading machine.

"I'm going to the house for lunch," he said. "I'll be back at one."

Oh, good, Lizzie thought, I get a whole hour for lunch. Her mouth watered, thinking of the good food she had packed in her insulated lunchbox that morning.

Lizzie washed her hands in the bathroom and went outside to eat her lunch. She found a freshly-mowed strip of grass that stretched beneath a towering oak tree.

RUNNING AROUND (AND SUCH)

Saturday Night Sandwiches

Makes 1 serving
Prep Time: 5 minutes • Cooking Time: 10-15 minutes

2 slices homemade
bread

butter

mayonnaise

cold roast chicken,
or turkey

sliced cheese

sliced tomatoes

salt, *optional*

1. Slice 2 pieces of bread, the thicker the better.

2. Spread butter on 1 side of each slice.

3. Place first slice in skillet, buttered side down.

4. Spread mayonnaise on other side of this slice.

5. Layer chicken or turkey, cheese, and tomatoes on mayonnaise-spread bread.

6. Sprinkle salt over tomato if you wish.

7. Top with second slice of bread, buttered side out.

Soups and Sandwiches

8. Fry over medium-low heat until first side is golden brown. Flip and continue to cook until second side is browned, the cheese is melted, and the other ingredients are warm.

9. Make as many of these sandwiches as you need.

> *"Come on, let's eat an early lunch. I'm starving. John isn't home today. He's helping his brother with hay and will eat there. So let's make those huge sandwiches like we used to make on Saturday evenings before church."*
>
> *They went to the kitchen, finding Swiss cheese, leftover chicken, tomatoes, and mayonnaise, which they slathered thickly on two slices of soft, chewy, homemade bread. Heating the griddle, they slowly toasted them while Mandy poured peppermint tea into two tall glasses, adding ice cubes from the refrigerator.*
>
> BIG DECISIONS

Hot Bologna and Cheese Sandwiches

Makes 16 servings
Prep Time: 20-30 minutes • Baking Time: 30 minutes

1-lb. piece bologna
¾ pound Velveeta cheese
2 Tbsp. chopped onions
1 Tbsp. sweet-pickle relish
½ cup Miracle Whip
salad dressing
¼ cup prepared mustard
16 sandwich rolls
aluminum foil

1. Grind or chop bologna, cheese, onions, and pickle relish together in a food mill or processor.

2. Add Miracle Whip and mustard. Stir well.

3. Spoon mixture into rolls.

4. Wrap sandwiches in aluminum foil. Place on baking sheet.

5. Heat oven to 300°, then turn off oven.

6. Put wrapped sandwiches in warmed oven for 30 minutes.

7. Serve warm.

*Jason slid onto the
bench beside Lizzie.
"I'm starved!" he said.
"Here. Take some
vegetable soup," Mam
said, hovering over him,
seeing that he had bread,
cheese, and sweet bologna.
Jason slapped bologna
on a slice of bread, threw
a piece of cheese on top,
smashed the second piece of
bread down on the cheese,
and stuffed half of the dry
sandwich into his mouth.*

WHEN STRAWBERRIES
BLOOM

Chicken Salad Sandwiches

Makes 2-4 servings
Prep Time: 20 minutes

2 cups cooked, cubed chicken breast

½ cup diced celery

¼ cup diced onion, *optional*

2 Tbsp. sugar

1 Tbsp. prepared mustard

¼ cup mayonnaise, *or* more *or* less

1. Chop chicken into small pieces. Place in mixing bowl.

2. Add celery and onion to chicken.

3. In separate bowl, combine sugar and mustard.

4. Stir into chicken.

5. Add just enough mayonnaise to moisten salad.

6. Serve in sandwich rolls or on a bed of lettuce.

Every day at lunch, they sat beneath the oak tree in the soft fragrant grass and shared the food they had packed. Dora's mother made soft, light-as-a-feather dinner rolls, which melted in Lizzie's mouth. Sometimes she also sent chicken salad made with great succulent chunks of white chicken and crispy pieces of celery and onion, mixed with creamy white mayonnaise.

RUNNING AROUND (AND SUCH)

Hot Dog Surprise

2 cups finely chopped hot dogs

2 cups finely chopped cooked ham

½ cup grated cheese of your choice

2 hard-boiled eggs,* chopped, *optional*

2 Tbsp. ketchup

2 Tbsp. pickle relish

½ onion, chopped

8 hot dog rolls

aluminum foil

* See page 35 for instructions about how to hard-boil eggs.

1. In medium bowl, mix hot dogs, ham, and cheese together.

2. Stir in eggs if you wish.

3. Fold in ketchup, relish, and onions.

4. Spoon mixture into hot dog rolls.

5. Wrap in aluminum foil. Lay stuffed rolls on baking sheet.

6. Bake at 350° for 10 minutes.

They stopped almost at the very peak of the mountain and had a long, delicious lunch, while the boys watered the horses at the spring which bubbled out of the rocks. It was a beautiful spot, one Lizzie would never forget, sitting surrounded by thick foliage that provided a brilliant background to the sweating horses.

WHEN STRAWBERRIES BLOOM

Toasted Cheese Sandwiches

Makes 1 serving
Prep Time: 5 minutes • *Cooking Time: 10 minutes*

2 slices homemade bread

butter

Velveeta cheese, sliced, *or* other cheese of your choice

fully cooked ham, roast beef, *or* bologna slices, *optional*

1. Slice two thick pieces of bread.

2. Butter both pieces on one side.

3. Place first slice of bread in frying pan, butter side down.

4. Top with cheese slices.

5. If you wish, add slices of fully cooked meat.

6. Top with second slice of bread, butter side up.

7. Fry over medium heat until golden brown on first side.

8. Flip. Fry until cheese melts and second side is golden brown.

9. Make as many of these sandwiches as you wish.

Food was such a comfort, such a cozy thing to have when worries assailed you. All you had to do was make a toasted cheese sandwich with plenty of butter, the Velveeta cheese dripping off your fingers as you ate it, and the world instantly became a better place.

BIG DECISIONS

O Christ, help Thou Thy people

Which follows Thee in all faithfulness...

Praise to Thee, God, on Thy throne

And also to Thy beloved Son

And to the Holy Ghost as well.

A HYMN FROM THE AUSBUND,
THE AMISH HYMNAL

Salads

Broccoli and Cauliflower Salad

Makes 10-12 servings
Prep Time: 30 minutes • Chilling Time: 2-3 hours

1 head broccoli

1 head cauliflower

½ pound shredded cheddar cheese

½-1 pound bacon, fried crisp and crumbled

1 cup chopped onions, *optional*

Dressing:

1 cup Miracle Whip salad dressing

1 cup sour cream

½ cup sugar

½ tsp. salt

1-2 tsp. vinegar

1. Chop broccoli and cauliflower into bite-sized pieces. Place in large bowl.

2. Stir in cheese, bacon, and onions if you wish.

3. In a separate bowl, combine dressing ingredients. Add vinegar to suit your taste.

4. Pour dressing over chopped vegetables.

5. Cover. Refrigerate at least 2 hours before serving.

With dinner over and the dishes done, the sisters worked outside with Mam, planting flowers in the new rock garden that Dat had built beside the house. Lizzie mixed peat moss into the topsoil while Mandy set up the rubber garden hose from the water hydrant by the barn.

WHEN STRAWBERRIES BLOOM

Mid-Summer Salad

Makes 10-12 servings
Prep Time: 20-30 minutes • Chilling Time: 2-3 hours, or overnight

1 quart cubed cucumbers
1 quart cubed tomatoes
½ quart chopped onions
Italian dressing

1. Combine all vegetables in a large bowl.

2. Pour Italian dressing over vegetables and stir to coat.

3. Cover. Refrigerate 2-3 hours, or overnight, before serving.

> When one of Mary's girls brought her supper tray, Lizzie opened her eyes wide as a smile of appreciation spread across her face. On the tray were two large yellow ears of corn, perfectly cooked, with a small dish of salad full of sliced tomatoes, carrots, and other fresh vegetables from Mary's garden.
>
> BIG DECISIONS

Lettuce with Cream Dressing

sometimes called "Cream Lettuce"

Makes 6-8 servings
Prep Time: 15-20 minutes

8 cups leaf lettuce, or baby lettuce, fresh from the garden

2 hard-boiled eggs, *optional*

Dressing:

½ cup sugar

¼ cup vinegar

⅓-½ cup sour cream

2-3 Tbsp. sliced green onions

1. Wash and dry lettuce. Place lettuce in large bowl.

2. Slice eggs and add to lettuce if you wish.

3. In separate bowl, combine dressing ingredients.

4. Just before serving, pour dressing over lettuce. Toss to coat.

So they walked the remainder of the way up the wooded hillside, the four of them in their bright dresses making a colorful scene against the backdrop of green leaves. As they neared Ben and Lydia King's home, they all remarked over Lydia's perfect flower beds and garden.

"She even has cabbage and lettuce that look absolutely healthy!" Rebecca said excitedly.

"What's so thrilling about that?" Lizzie wanted to know.

"Oh, a lot. We're moving onto a produce farm, you know, so I'll be busy helping Reuben with all kinds of vegetables and things. Imagine! We'll have about a hundred times the amount of this garden."

BIG DECISIONS

Carrot-Raisin Salad

Makes 4-5 servings
Prep Time: 20 minutes

2½ cups shredded carrots
(approximately
3 large carrots)

½ cup chopped celery

½ cup raisins

½ cup mayonnaise

1 tsp. lemon juice

1. In medium bowl, mix together carrots, celery, and raisins.

2. In a small bowl, mix together mayonnaise and lemon juice.

3. Pour dressing over salad ingredients and mix together gently but well.

4. Cover. Refrigerate until ready to serve.

Cucumber and Onion Salad

Makes 4 servings
Prep Time: 20 minutes

2 large cucumbers, sliced, and peeled if you wish

1 large onion, sliced

¾ cup sour cream

3 Tbsp. vinegar

2 Tbsp. sugar

dash of salt

dash of pepper

1. Combine cucumbers and onions in good-sized mixing bowl.

2. In separate bowl, mix sour cream, vinegar, sugar, salt, and pepper together.

3. Pour dressing over cucumbers and onions. Mix well.

4. Cover and refrigerate until ready to serve.

Layered Green Salad

Makes 10-12 servings

Prep Time: 30 minutes • Chilling Time: 6-8 hours, or overnight

1 head iceberg lettuce, chopped

1 cup chopped celery

4 hard-boiled eggs, sliced *or* grated

8 slices cooked bacon, crumbled

1-lb. bag frozen peas

1 cup shredded carrots

2 cups mayonnaise

1 cup shredded cheese of your choice

1. In a 9" × 13" pan, make a layer of lettuce, followed by a layer of celery, a layer of eggs, a layer of bacon, a layer of peas, and a layer of carrots.

2. Spread mayonnaise over vegetables.

3. Sprinkle cheese on top.

4. Do not toss! Cover.

5. Refrigerate 6-8 hours, or overnight.

6. Toss before serving, or serve layered.

> *Lizzie nodded, but she couldn't help but wonder how God would direct her if there weren't any boys nearby. Before she could ask Mam more about God's will and future husbands, Mommy Glick called them to dinner. Lizzie followed Mam into the dining room where the table was covered with food.*
>
> RUNNING AROUND (AND SUCH)

Cole Slaw

1 large head cabbage, shredded

1 cup chopped celery

½ medium onion, chopped

1 green bell pepper, chopped

Dressing:

1½ cups sugar

½-¾ cup vinegar

1 tsp. celery seed

½ tsp. mustard seed

2 tsp. salt

1. In large bowl, mix together cabbage, celery, onion, and pepper.

2. In separate bowl, stir together sugar, vinegar, celery seed, mustard seed, and salt.

3. Stir dressing into vegetables.

4. Cover. Refrigerate for 2-3 hours before serving to allow flavors to blend.

Oh, yes, and in the afternoon whole stalks of celery to snack on were placed in tall vases and set on the tables.

"Why celery?" Lizzie asked, as she scrubbed yet another piece.

"Because over a hundred years ago, our ancestors served whatever was in the garden at the end of the season at their weddings. That's why we have chicken filling, mashed potatoes, celery, and cole slaw. The cabbage, potatoes, and celery all come from the late harvest," Joshua informed her proudly.

"They grew the chickens in the garden too, huh?" Lizzie cracked.

WHEN STRAWBERRIES BLOOM

Creamy Cole Slaw

Makes 4-6 servings
Prep Time: 30 minutes • *Chilling Time: 2-3 hours*

½ head cabbage, shredded

2 carrots, grated

2 Tbsp. parsley

Dressing:

¼ cup vinegar

¼ cup sugar

½ cup mayonnaise

2 tsp. celery seed

1. Place cabbage, carrots, and parsley in a medium bowl.

2. In a separate bowl, mix vinegar, sugar, mayonnaise, and celery seed together.

3. Add dressing to vegetables. Stir.

4. Cover and refrigerate 2-3 hours to allow flavors to blend.

Lizzie and Stephen were told their dinner was ready in less than half an hour after the service was over. The wooden benches where people were seated during the ceremony were placed around the tables, tablecloths were put on, and dozens of hands passed out plates, water pitchers, rolls, butter, jelly, applesauce, cole slaw, filled doughnuts, trays of cookies, fruit, and hot platters of food before the guests were again seated.

Lizzie tried hard to keep a mature, serene expression on her face, but her smile just kept sliding out of control. She was deep-down, really happy, genuinely pleased to have become Stephen's wife, to spend this wonderful day of celebration as the honored guest who sat in the most important seat, the eck, *or corner.*

BIG DECISIONS

Potato Salad

Makes 6-8 servings
Prep Time: 30 minutes • Cooking Time: 20 minutes
Chilling Time: 4 hours for potatoes; 3-4 hours,
or overnight, for completed salad

6 medium to large
potatoes, unpeeled

4-6 hard-boiled eggs,
grated

½ cup chopped celery

¼-½ cup chopped
onion

Dressing:

1½ cups mayonnaise

¾ cup sugar

¼ cup milk

⅛ cup vinegar

3 Tbsp. prepared
mustard

2 tsp. salt

1. Boil potatoes until slightly
   soft, but not too soft. Drain.

2. Chill potatoes until
   completely cold, to make
   grating easier.

3. Peel. Grate cold potatoes into
   good-sized mixing bowl.

4. Gently fold in grated hard-
   boiled eggs and chopped
   celery and onions.

5. In a separate bowl, combine
   dressing ingredients and mix
   well.

6. Pour dressing over potato
   mixture. Stir to combine.

7. Cover. Chill 3-4 hours, or
   overnight, and then serve.

> *After dinner, Lizzie went up to her room. She found her Bible in her nightstand drawer and carried it with her as she climbed into bed. She propped up both pillows and leaned back against the headboard. She bent her head over her Bible in her lap.*
>
> RUNNING AROUND
> (AND SUCH)

Macaroni Salad

Makes 4 servings
Prep Time: 20 minutes • Cooking Time: 8-10 minutes
Chilling time: 3-4 hours, or overnight

2 heaping cups
uncooked
macaroni

½ cup grated
carrots

½ cup diced celery

2 hard-boiled
eggs, chopped

¼ cup chopped
onions

1 tsp. parsley

Dressing:

1 cup mayonnaise

1 Tbsp. prepared
mustard

½ tsp. salt

1 Tbsp. vinegar

1. Cook macaroni according to package directions.

2. Drain. Cool in large mixing bowl.

3. Add carrots, celery, eggs, onion, and parsley to macaroni in mixing bowl.

4. In separate bowl, stir together mayonnaise, mustard, salt, and vinegar.

5. Combine dressing with pasta and vegetables.

6. Cover. Refrigerate 3-4 hours, or overnight, before serving.

"Mayonnaise isn't fattening."
"It is."
"No, I know it isn't."
"Lizzie!"
"It isn't." Lizzie scooped a large spoonful of macaroni salad onto her plate, her second helping, before taking a large bite.
RUNNING AROUND (AND SUCH)

Red Beet Eggs

Makes 12 servings

Prep Time: 30 minutes • *Chilling Time: 24 hours*

12 eggs

1 quart pickled
red beets

1. To make hard-boiled eggs, place eggs in saucepan. Cover with water.

2. Bring to a full, rolling boil.

3. Turn off burner.

4. With lid on, let eggs stand for 10 minutes.

5. Cool immediately under cold running water.

6. Peel eggs. Place in large bowl. (Eggs should remain whole.)

7. Pour quart of red beets, with juice, over peeled eggs.

8. Cover. Refrigerate for 24 hours before serving. Eggs will turn a deep rose-color.

Applesauce, dark green sweet pickles, and red beet eggs completed the meal.

RUNNING AROUND (AND SUCH)

Apple Salad

Makes 6-8 servings
Prep Time: 30 minutes
Cooling Time: 20 minutes • *Cooking Time: 5-10 minutes*

20-oz. can crushed pineapple

water

2 eggs, beaten

1½ cups sugar

2 Tbsp. flour

¼ stick (2 Tbsp.) butter, cut into chunks

1 tsp. vinegar

1 tsp. vanilla

6-8 peeled apples, chopped *or* grated

3 bananas, sliced

1. To make the dressing, drain pineapple and reserve the juice.

2. Add water to pineapple juice to equal 2 cups.

3. Combine pineapple juice, eggs, sugar, and flour in medium saucepan.

4. Cook until thickened, stirring continually to prevent sticking.

5. Stir in butter, vinegar, and vanilla.

6. Allow to cool.

7. In separate bowl, combine apples, bananas, and pineapple.

8. Pour dressing over fruit and stir to combine.

9. Cover and chill until ready to serve.

Lizzie had packed a bag with potato chips, homemade dill pickles, peanut butter chocolate chip cookies, and large red apples, polished until they looked like a picture in a storybook.

WHEN STRAWBERRIES
BLOOM

Christmas Salad

Makes 12-15 servings
Prep Time: 20 minutes • Chilling Time: 7-8 hours, total

Layer 1:

4 cups
boiling water

2 3.4-oz. pkgs.
lime gelatin

15-oz. can crushed
pineapple, drained
but with juice
reserved

Layer 2:

2 envelopes
Dream Whip
topping mix

8-oz. pkg.
cream cheese,
softened to room
temperature

Layer 3:

1½ cups
pineapple juice

1 cup sugar

3 egg yolks

3 Tbsp. flour

pinch of salt

lettuce leaves

1. To make the first layer, bring water to boil in medium-sized saucepan.

2. Stir gelatin into boiling water.

3. Place saucepan containing dissolved gelatin in refrigerator. Allow to chill until just starting to set.

4. Drain crushed pineapple, saving juice.

5. Stir drained pineapple into chilled, partially-set gelatin.

6. Pour mixture into 9" × 13" pan. Cover and return to fridge until stiff.

7. To make the second layer, mix whipped topping according to package directions.

8. Add cream cheese in chunks to whipped topping, stirring until smooth.

9. When gelatin is firm, spread layer of whipped topping/cream cheese mixture on top.

10. Cover and return gelatin to fridge so second layer can firm up.

11. For the third layer, add water to reserved pineapple juice so it equals 1½ cups.

12. Separate the eggs. (Save whites for another use.)

13. Combine pineapple juice, sugar, egg yolks, flour, and salt in medium saucepan. Cook over medium heat, stirring constantly, until thickened.

14. When first two layers of salad are firm, spread third layer on top.

15. Refrigerate 2-3 hours, or until all 3 layers are firm, before serving.

16. Cut into squares. Place lettuce leaves on individual salad plates. Top each with a square of Christmas Salad.

> *Each year she would start by looking through all of her cookbooks, particularly her red hardcover Betty Crocker one. Then out would come her gray metal recipe box with the tattered yellow recipe cards that held all the wonders of Christmas.*
>
> WHEN STRAWBERRIES BLOOM

Jello Mold

Makes 8 servings

Prep Time: 20 minutes   •   Cooling Time: 30-45 minutes
Chilling Time: approximately 3 hours

1 cup boiling water

2 3.4-oz. pkgs. gelatin,
any flavor

8-oz. pkg. cream
cheese, softened

12-oz. can evaporated
milk

8-oz. container frozen
whipped topping,
thawed

1. Bring water to a boil in small saucepan.

2. Dissolve gelatin in boiling water.

3. Cool to room temperature.

4. In a large bowl, beat cream cheese until creamy. Stir in evaporated milk until well blended.

5. Fold in whipped topping.

6. Mix cooled gelatin with creamy mixture.

7. Pour into gelatin mold, or into individual serving dishes.

8. Refrigerate 3 hours, or until firm.

> *They served it on every table throughout the house, with small squares of red and green Jell-O on top, because their wedding was so close to Christmas.*
>
> BIG DECISIONS

Vegetables

Baked Corn

Makes 4-6 servings
Prep Time: 15 minutes • Baking Time: 40-45 minutes

2 eggs

2 cups corn

1 cup milk

⅔ cup crushed
cracker crumbs

3 Tbsp. butter, melted

½ tsp. salt

¼ tsp., *or less,* pepper

1 Tbsp. sugar

¼ cup minced onion

1. In a small bowl, beat eggs.

2. In a separate bowl, combine all other ingredients.

3. Add eggs and mix well.

4. Pour into 1½-quart greased casserole dish. Bake at 350° for 40-45 minutes, or until knife inserted in center of dish comes out clean.

Lizzie was sincerely thankful that it was 12 o'clock and time for lunch. She was almost weak with hunger, since she had been too nervous to eat much breakfast that morning. As she went down the stairs, the delicious smells from the kitchen made her mouth water. Mary Beiler must be a good cook, she thought happily.

"You can wash the children's hands in the bathroom," Mary said. "Abner, go with Liz. She'll wash your 'patties!'"

Liz! Didn't that sound classy! Imagine how nice it would be if everyone called her Liz! That would make it seem as if she was already 16 years old.

RUNNING AROUND (AND SUCH)

Corn Fritters

Makes 4 servings

Prep Time: 10 minutes • *Cooking Time: 10-15 minutes*

2 cups fresh corn; *or*
frozen corn, thawed;
or canned corn,
drained well

2 eggs

¼ cup flour

1 tsp. salt

⅛ tsp. pepper

1 tsp. baking powder

2 tsp. cream

½ cup vegetable oil

confectioners sugar,
optional

1. In medium bowl, combine corn, eggs, flour, salt, pepper, and baking powder.

2. Stir in cream.

3. Pour ½ cup vegetable oil into large skillet.

4. When oil is hot, drop teaspoonfuls of corn mixture into oil.

5. Fry until golden brown and crispy on both sides.

6. Before serving, sprinkle with confectioners sugar if you wish.

> *They froze tiny little bags of corn, lima beans, and peas for Emma, in bags only big enough for two people. Emma beamed and giggled as she put one cup of vegetables in each bag, saying how cozy that would be, cooking supper for Joshua in their old farmhouse.*
>
> WHEN STRAWBERRIES BLOOM

Corn on the Cob

Makes 4 ears of corn
Prep Time: 10 minutes • Cooking Time: 15 minutes

4 ears of fresh corn, husked and silked

1. Place ears of corn in 8-10 quart stockpot.

2. Cover corn with cold water.

3. Cover pot. Bring water to boil.

4. Boil uncovered for 2-5 minutes, depending on the size of the ears and their kernels.

5. Turn burner off and let stand in hot water 10 minutes.

When Lizzie began to eat, she wished there were two slices of bread on her tray and two more ears of corn.

BIG DECISIONS

Barbecued Green Beans

Makes 6-8 servings
Prep Time: 20 minutes • Baking Time: 1-1½ hours

½ pound bacon

¼ cup chopped onion

¾ tsp. salt

½ cup sugar

¾ cup ketchup

¾ tsp. Worcestershire sauce

4 cups fresh, *or* canned, green beans

1. Cut bacon into bite-sized pieces.

2. Place bacon and onion in medium skillet. Fry until bacon is crispy.

3. Remove bacon and allow to drain.

4. In separate bowl, stir together browned onion, salt, sugar, ketchup, and Worcestershire sauce.

5. Add beans and bacon and mix well.

6. Pour into greased 3- to 3½-quart baking dish.

7. Cover. Bake at 300° for 1-1½ hours. (Fresh beans will require a longer cooking time than canned beans. Check after 1 hour to see if beans are as tender as you like them.)

Green Bean Casserole

Makes 6 servings
Prep Time: 20 minutes • *Baking Time: 40 minutes*

2 16-oz. pkgs. frozen green beans

10¾-oz. can cream of chicken, celery, *or* mushroom soup

½ cup milk

⅛ tsp. pepper

2.8-oz. can French-fried onions, *optional*

1. Cook green beans in small amount of water, covered, for approximately 10 minutes in saucepan. Drain. Green beans will be slightly crunchy.

2. In large bowl, mix soup, milk, and pepper together until smooth. Stir in beans.

3. Place mixture into greased 2- to 2½-quart baking dish.

4. Sprinkle with onions.

5. Bake at 350° for 40 minutes.

Mandy was not allowed to see what Emma and the cousins were doing, because it was all a surprise for her when she sat at the corner table the day she was married.

The women cut butter into fancy wedding-bell shapes, covering it carefully with plastic wrap and refrigerating it for the big day. They made special Jell-O dishes, fruit dip, and all kinds of delicious food for the bride and groom.

"What beautiful china!" Emma gasped.

BIG DECISIONS

Barbecued Beans

2 medium onions, chopped

¼ stick (2 Tbsp.) butter

1 Tbsp. vinegar

2 Tbsp. brown sugar

1 Tbsp. flour

1 cup ketchup

1 cup cut-up, cooked ham, *or* 8 slices bacon, cooked crisp and crumbled, *optional*

2 15 ½-oz. cans, *or* 4 cups home-canned Great Northern, *or* navy, beans, undrained

1. Cook onions in butter in skillet until soft. Remove from heat.

2. In a large bowl, mix together vinegar, brown sugar, flour, and ketchup.

3. Stir onions into sauce.

4. Add ham or bacon if you wish.

5. Add beans and mix well.

6. Pour into greased 2-quart baking dish.

7. Cover and bake for 45 minutes at 350°.

8. Uncover. Bake an additional 15 minutes.

TIP:

If sauce seems too thick in Step 2, add extra ketchup.

> *Lizzie also admired the baked beans that had been baking most of the forenoon and now were rich with tomato sauce and bacon. Bits of onion floated among the beans, and steam wafted from the granite roaster.*
>
> RUNNING AROUND
> (AND SUCH)

Crusty Baked Potatoes

Makes 6 servings

Prep Time: 15 minutes • Baking Time: 1 hour

6 medium potatoes

1 cup crushed
cracker crumbs

half a stick (4 Tbsp.
butter), melted

1 tsp. seasoned salt

1. Peel potatoes. Rinse and cut in half.

2. In a shallow dish, combine cracker crumbs and melted butter.

3. Grease a 9" × 13" baking dish.

4. Roll potatoes halves in cracker crumbs until well coated.

5. Place potatoes in baking dish, cut side up.

6. Sprinkle with seasoned salt.

7. Bake at 350° for 1 hour, or until soft.

Throughout the summer, their friendship deepened. Lizzie looked forward to her days with Julie. One day while they sat side by side eating lunch, Julie told Lizzie that she and her husband, Gary, had decided to give their lives to God and join the River Brethren. They would dress plain, as their parents did.

Lizzie blinked, surprised. She could see Julie was very serious.

"You mean you'll dress with a covering and a long dress? Completely different than now?"

Julie nodded soberly.

"But then…You'll be different? You won't laugh and talk the way you do now?"

Julie laughed. "Of course I will!"

BIG DECISIONS

Potluck Potatoes

Makes 10-12 servings
Prep Time: 30 minutes • Cooking Time: 20-30 minutes
Chilling Time: 5-6 hours, or overnight • Baking Time: 45-50 minutes

2-3 lbs. potatoes

1½ sticks (¾ cup) butter, *divided*

½ cup chopped onions

1 tsp. salt

¼ tsp. pepper

10¾-oz. can cream of chicken soup

1 pint sour cream

2 cups cubed Velveeta cheese

2 cups crushed cornflakes

1. Peel potatoes. Place in saucepan with about 2" of water.

2. Cover. Cook over medium heat until soft. Drain.

3. Allow potatoes to cool in fridge until completely cold, 5-6 hours, or overnight. (Cold potatoes shred far easier than those that aren't.)

4. Grease a 9" × 13" baking dish.

5. When potatoes are thoroughly cold, shred and place in greased baking dish.

6. In a small saucepan, combine ½ cup butter, onions, salt, pepper, soup, sour cream, and cheese.

7. Stirring occasionally, cook on medium heat until cheese is melted.

8. Pour cheese sauce over potatoes.

9. Bake at 350° for 15 minutes.

10. Melt remaining ¼ cup butter. Combine with crushed cornflakes.

11. Sprinkle cornflakes over potatoes and return to oven.

12. Bake 30-40 more minutes.

> *Sometimes she would put a package of cheese crackers in her* kaevly *and eat them while she fed Laura, because it got late and she became very hungry. The thing was, when they served lunch, she was never able to sit at the first women's table because they were seated according to their ages. So she had to wait with the younger women and girls till the older ones had eaten. It seemed as if that table of older women always took their time, drinking coffee and talking way too much.*
>
> BIG DECISIONS

Scalloped Potatoes

Makes 10-12 servings
Prep Time: 30 minutes
Cooking Time: 30-40 minutes • Baking Time: 1 hour

8-10 medium potatoes

1 medium onion, chopped

½ stick (4 Tbsp.) butter

2-3 cups milk

¾-1 tsp. salt

¼ tsp. pepper

1 cup water

1 Tbsp. flour

1 cup shredded cheese of your choice

1. Peel potatoes and cook in water over medium heat until medium soft, but allow for a little crunch.

2. Meanwhile, grease a 9" × 13" baking dish.

3. When potatoes are cool, slice into greased baking dish.

4. In medium-sized saucepan, cook onion in butter until soft.

5. Add milk to onions.

6. Add salt and pepper.

7. In a separate bowl, stir water and flour into a smooth paste.

8. Add flour mixture to onion mixture. Over medium heat, stir continually until sauce becomes creamy and thickened.

9. Remove from heat and stir in cheese until melted.

10. Pour sauce over potatoes and mix together.

11. Bake at 350° for 1 hour.

> *Lizzie and Stephen were told their dinner was ready in less than half an hour after the service was over. The wooden benches where people were seated during the ceremony were placed around the tables, tablecloths were put on, and dozens of hands passed out plates, water pitchers, rolls, butter, jelly, applesauce, cole slaw, filled doughnuts, trays of cookies, fruit, and hot platters of food before the guests were again seated.*
>
> BIG DECISIONS

Mashed Potatoes

4-6 large potatoes

1-1½ cups milk

1 tsp. salt

½ stick (4 Tbsp.) butter

8-oz. pkg. cream cheese, softened, *or* 1 cup sour cream, *optional*

1-1½ cups milk

1. Peel potatoes and cut into large pieces.

2. Place potatoes in saucepan. Add about 2" of water. Cover.

3. Bring to boil over medium heat. Reduce heat, but allow potatoes and water to simmer, cooking until potatoes are very soft. Check to make sure potatoes do not cook dry.

4. While potatoes are cooking, place milk in saucepan. Heat just to boiling point, but do not boil. A skin will form when the milk gets as hot as it should be.

5. Drain water from cooked potatoes.

6. Mash potatoes with potato masher or wire whisk.

7. Add salt and butter and continue mashing.

8. Add cream cheese or sour cream if you wish and continue mashing.

9. Add milk until potatoes are creamy.

> *The boys came in for supper, filling their plates before sitting in the living room to eat. The girls ate around the kitchen table, laughing about the lumpy gravy on the mashed potatoes.*
>
> WHEN STRAWBERRIES
> BLOOM

Potato Patties

Makes 3-4 servings

Prep Time: 10 minutes • *Cooking Time: 15 minutes*

1 cup leftover mashed potatoes

2 eggs

¼ tsp. salt, *optional*

½ cup flour

1 tsp. baking powder

¼-½ cup vegetable oil

1. In medium bowl, beat together mashed potatoes, eggs, salt if you wish, flour, and baking powder.

2. Pour vegetable oil into medium-sized skillet.

3. When oil is hot, drop potato mixture by teaspoonfuls into skillet.

4. Fry until golden brown on both sides.

5. Serve immediately with gravy or pancake syrup.

Onion Patties

Makes 6-8 servings

Prep Time: 15 minutes • *Cooking Time: 15 minutes*

¾ cup flour

2 tsp. baking powder

1 Tbsp. sugar

1 tsp. salt

1 Tbsp. cornmeal

2½ cups minced onion

milk, just enough to hold batter together

½ cup vegetable oil, *or* lard

ketchup *and/or* Ranch dressing

1. In medium bowl, mix together flour, baking powder, sugar, salt, cornmeal, and onion.

2. Add milk slowly, just enough to hold batter together. Stir continually to make sure batter is not too thin.

3. Heat vegetable oil or lard in a skillet.

4. Drop batter by teaspoonfuls into hot oil.

5. Fry until golden brown on both sides.

6. Serve with ketchup and/or Ranch dressing for dipping.

Sweet Potato Casserole

Makes 6 servings
Prep Time: 15 minutes
Cooking Time: 20-30 minutes • Baking Time: 35-45 minutes

3 medium to large
sweet potatoes,
peeled

2 eggs

½ cup milk

¼ cup sugar

½ tsp. salt

½ stick (4 Tbsp.)
butter, melted

½ tsp. vanilla

Crumbs:

½ cup sugar

1 cup chopped nuts

⅓ cup flour

⅓ stick (5⅓ Tbsp.)
butter, melted

1. Cook potatoes in saucepan in about 2" water, covered, until very tender.

2. Drain potatoes. Mash until smooth.

3. In large mixing bowl mix together eggs, milk, sugar, salt, butter, and vanilla.

4. Stir potatoes into egg mixture.

5. Spoon into greased 2-quart baking dish.

6. To make crumbs, combine sugar, nuts, flour, and butter in a small bowl.

7. Sprinkle crumbs over potatoes.

8. Bake at 350° for 35-45 minutes, or until heated through.

She heard the kitchen door banging and wondered if it was already lunchtime. She sure was getting hungry, but it seemed too early to be noon. Then she heard the stairs squeak in protest as Mam came up at a fast pace. She appeared at the doorway, her scarf coming loose, her hair windblown, and a hand over her chest as she struggled to regain her breath.

"What is it, Mam?" Lizzie scrambled to her feet, her face ashen.

"It's Mandy! She had a doctor's appointment today, and they have a pair of twin girls!"

"No!" Lizzie screeched.

"Yes, they do!"

BIG DECISIONS

Zucchini Casserole

Makes 6-8 servings
Prep Time: 15-20 minutes • Baking Time: 45 minutes

3 eggs
¼ cup vegetable oil
½ cup flour
½ tsp. salt
1½ tsp. baking powder
½ cup grated cheese of your choice
¼ cup parsley
½ cup chopped onions
2 cups unpeeled grated zucchini

1. In medium bowl, beat eggs and oil together.

2. Stir in flour, salt, and baking powder.

3. Add cheese, parsley, onion, and zucchini.

4. Mix well.

5. Pour into greased 2-quart casserole dish. Bake at 350° for 45 minutes.

After Lizzie had eaten everything, Barbara brought a pretty glass dish piled high with ice-cold chunks of watermelon. The fruit was delicious. So good, in fact, that Lizzie resolved to turn her own dry, little hilltop garden into a garden just like Mary's. She would plant plots of herbs and teas and have different flowers and vegetables all growing in neat squares, one complementing the other like pictures of gardens in seed catalogs.

BIG DECISIONS

Cooked Celery

Makes 4 servings
Prep Time: 10 minutes • Cooking Time: 20 minutes

1½ cups
chopped celery

1 Tbsp. butter

1 Tbsp. flour

1 Tbsp. sugar

1 Tbsp. vinegar

1 egg, beaten

½ cup water

1. Place celery in medium saucepan.

2. Cover celery with water and cook until soft. Drain off water. Set celery aside.

3. In separate saucepan, melt butter.

4. Stir in flour, sugar, and vinegar.

5. Cook slowly until mixture starts to boil.

6. Reduce heat and allow to simmer a few minutes.

7. Add beaten egg and water.

8. Allow to boil lightly until slightly thickened.

9. Stir thickened sauce into celery and serve.

There was the usual happy banter as the food was prepared. Lizzie's aunts baked pies, cooked tapioca pudding, washed the celery, and baked bread until the whole house was a regular beehive of activity. BIG DECISIONS

Then I commended mirth,

*because a man hath no better
    thing under the sun,*

*than to eat, and to drink, and to
    be merry:*

*for that shall abide with him of
    his labour the days of his life,*

*which God giveth him under
    the sun.*

ECCLESIASTES 8:15

Desserts

Apple Crumb Pie

Makes 1 9" pie, or 8 slices
Prep Time: 25 minutes • Baking Time: 40 minutes

1½ cups water

1 cup brown sugar

1 tsp. cinnamon

1 Tbsp. cornstarch

1 Tbsp. butter, softened

2-3 cups grated apples

9" unbaked pie crust (see recipe for Pie Crust on page 215)

Crumbs:

1 cup brown sugar

1 cup dry oatmeal

½ cup flour

3 Tbsp. butter

1. In a medium saucepan, combine water, brown sugar, cinnamon, and cornstarch. Cook over medium heat, stirring frequently until smooth and slightly thickened.

2. Remove saucepan from heat. Stir in butter and apples.

3. Pour into unbaked pie crust.

4. To make the crumbs, stir brown sugar, oatmeal, and flour together in a good-sized mixing bowl.

5. Using a pastry cutter, or 2 forks, cut butter into mixture until small crumbs form.

6. Sprinkle crumbs evenly over pie.

7. Bake at 425° for 10 minutes.

8. Reduce heat to 350° and continue baking for 30 minutes.

> *Lizzie sat on the bench along the wall, eating a piece of apple crumb pie with milk before she went to feed the horses and help with the milking. She was perfectly relaxed since she had resolved not to go work as a* maud.
>
> RUNNING AROUND (AND SUCH)

Peach Pie

Makes 1 9" pie, or 8 slices
Prep Time: 15-20 minutes
Cooling Time: 20-30 minutes • Baking Time: 30-40 minutes

¾ cup sugar

¼ tsp. salt

2 Tbsp. Clear-Jel

⅓ cup water

1 quart peaches,
peeled and cut into
bite-size pieces

1 9" unbaked pie
crust with top crust
(see recipe for
Pie Crust on page 215)

1. In a small bowl, combine sugar, salt, Clear-Jel, and water. Mix together well.

2. Place peaches in medium saucepan over low to medium heat.

3. When peaches are hot, gently stir in Clear-Jel mixture.

4. Continue heating, stirring continually, until mixture comes to a boil. Allow to cook until thickened, continuing to stir.

5. Cool until warm but not hot.

6. Pour into unbaked pie crust.

7. Roll out crust to top pie. Lift over filled pie and pinch edges to secure. Cut 6 slashes across top crust to allow steam to escape.

8. Bake at 425° for 10 minutes.

9. Reduce heat to 375° and continue baking for 20-30 minutes, or until filling is bubbly and crust is browned.

> *Later at home, after supper was eaten, Mam lingered around the table with Mandy and Lizzie. She put another piece of peach pie on her plate, added a bit of ice cream and said, "Mmm!"*
>
> *Lizzie grinned at Mam. "I know. That pie is still warm. Did you ever notice how it is with pie and ice cream? You don't always have quite enough ice cream to finish your pie, then you don't have quite enough pie to finish your ice cream, and it just goes on and on."*
>
> *Mam laughed. "Oh, I know exactly what you mean. I could eat that whole pie!"*
>
> WHEN STRAWBERRIES BLOOM

Blueberry Pie

Makes 1 9" pie, or 8 slices
Prep Time: 15-20 minutes
Cooling Time: 2-3 hours • Baking Time: 40 minutes

¾-1 cup sugar

¼ tsp. salt

2 Tbsp. Clear-Jel

½ cup water

1 quart blueberries,
fresh *or* canned

9" unbaked 2-layer
pie crust
(see page 215 for
Pie Crust recipe)

1. In a small bowl, combine sugar, salt, Clear-Jel, and water.

2. Drain blueberries (unless using fresh berries). Pour berries into medium saucepan and heat.

3. When berries are hot, gently stir in Clear-Jel mixture.

4. Continue heating until the mixture boils and thickens slightly.

5. Cool to room temperature.

6. Pour into unbaked pie crust.

7. Roll out remaining pastry to make pastry lid for pie. Place on top of pie. Cut slits to allow steam to escape.

8. Bake at 425° for 10 minutes.

9. Reduce heat to 375°. Continue baking for 30 minutes, or until blueberry filling is bubbly and top crust is well browned.

Dat and Jason were making popcorn. Lizzie was instantly hungry. Mam had made a pitcher of ice-cold chocolate milk and put out pumpkin whoopie pies and blueberry pie. Lizzie sat in a chair, smiling at Emma, feeling quite pleased because everyone had been worried.

"Where were you, Lizzie?" Mam asked.

"In my room."

"What were you doing?"

"Reading."

"Didn't you hear us looking for you?"

"Hm-mm."

"I bet you did," Emma said.

RUNNING AROUND
(AND SUCH)

Pumpkin Pie

Makes 2 9" pies, or 16 slices

Prep Time: 20 minutes • Baking Time: 40 minutes

1¼ cups sugar

1 Tbsp. flour

1½ tsp. cinnamon

½ tsp. salt

3 eggs, separated

1¼ cups canned pumpkin

12-oz. can evaporated milk

1½ tsp. vanilla

1½ cups milk, heated

2 9" unbaked pie crusts

1. In medium bowl, combine sugar, flour, cinnamon, and salt.

2. Using two other bowls, separate eggs.

3. Add yolks to the sugar mixture. Stir with a whisk.

4. Stir in pumpkin.

5. Add evaporated milk and vanilla.

6. Heat 1½ cups milk on stove, stirring constantly until milk is hot, but not boiling.

7. With a wire whisk, slightly beat egg whites.

8. Add milk and egg whites to the pumpkin mixture and stir.

9. Divide evenly between 2 unbaked pie crusts.

10. Bake at 425° for 10 minutes.

11. Reduce heat to 350° and continue baking for 30 minutes.

12. Remove from oven when pie is still slightly shaky in the middle.

13. Cool to room temperature before slicing and serving.

> So Lizzie ate a large piece of pumpkin pie for dessert, free of guilt, because it seemed as if Mam was on her side. That one piece was not quite enough for her, so when they were clearing the table, Lizzie ate another piece, only smaller, when Emma wasn't looking. That left kind of a yucky sweet taste in her mouth, so when she took the pie back to the pantry, she got a handful of stick pretzels from the jar. Emma came into the kitchen just as Lizzie grabbed another handful of pretzels.
>
> "Lizzie," she said. "Are you still eating?"
>
> RUNNING AROUND (AND SUCH)

Butterscotch Pie

Makes 2 9" pies, or 16 slices
Prep Time: 20-25 minutes
Cooling Time: 1 hour • *Chilling Time: 3-4 hours*

1st part:

1 cup brown sugar
3 Tbsp. butter
1 cup water
1 tsp. vanilla
¼ tsp. baking soda
¼ tsp. salt

2nd part:

1 cup brown sugar
3 Tbsp. flour
3 Tbsp. cornstarch
3 eggs
4½ cups milk

2 9" baked pie crusts
(see page 215 for
Pie Crust recipe)

1. To make the first part of the pie, place brown sugar and butter into a good-sized saucepan. Bring to a boil, stirring constantly.

2. Boil mixture 5 minutes, continuing to stir.

3. Remove from heat and add water.

4. Stir in vanilla, baking soda, and salt. Set aside.

5. To make the second part of the pie, stir together brown sugar, flour, cornstarch, and eggs in separate bowl.

6. Gradually add milk, whisking constantly so that mixture is smooth.

7. Add second part to the first part in the saucepan. Over medium heat, cook, stirring constantly, until mixture is thickened.

8. Pour into baked pie crusts.

9. Cool to room temperature. Then cover and refrigerate 3-4 hours, or until butterscotch filling is set and can be sliced.

> *It wasn't that the family couldn't survive without Lizzie's help, she knew. It was just sad to think that it was all over now. Her new life with Stephen would begin this evening when they were all alone in the funny little unfinished basement on the hill behind the farm. Lizzie looked up to see Mandy gazing intently in her direction. She lowered her eyes, willing herself to finish this last piece of butterscotch pie.*
>
> BIG DECISIONS

Shoofly Pie

Makes 2 9" pies, or 16 slices
Prep Time: 20 minutes • Baking Time: 1 hour

Crumbs:

3 cups pastry flour

¾ cup brown sugar

½ tsp. baking soda

½ tsp. baking powder

1 stick (8 Tbsp.) butter, at room temperature

Gooey Bottom:

1½ cups brown sugar

1 small egg

1 cup sweet molasses

1½ cups hot water

½ tsp. baking soda

2 9" unbaked pie crusts

1. To make the crumbs, stir flour, brown sugar, baking soda, and baking powder together in a good-sized mixing bowl.

2. Using a pastry cutter, or 2 forks, cut butter into mixture.

3. Stir with a fork until mixture forms soft crumbs.

4. Using another mixing bowl, stir together all ingredients for the gooey bottom.

5. Stir 2 cups crumbs into gooey bottom mixture. (Reserve remaining crumbs.)

6. Divide gooey bottom mixture between 2 unbaked pie crusts.

7. Sprinkle evenly with reserved crumbs.

8. Bake at 400° for 15 minutes.

9. Reduce heat to 350° and continue baking for 45 minutes.

She was so hungry after her morning's work that she ate and ate without even thinking of calories or her weight. She couldn't wait to cut a fresh piece of shoofly pie and pour a mug of steaming hot chocolate over it. Shoofly pie was one of her favorite foods. Mam's shoofly pies were almost as good as Mommy Glick's, with a thick brown sugar and molasses goo on the bottom and a soft crumb cake on top.

RUNNING AROUND (AND SUCH)

When they finished eating the main part of the meal, Lizzie and Mandy helped themselves to pieces of shoofly pie and sat on the steps of the porch together. They each bit off the very tips of their pieces.

"No one else in the whole world can make shoofly pies like Mommy Glick," Lizzie said.

Mandy nodded, her mouth full as she ate her way through the whole delicious piece.

RUNNING AROUND (AND SUCH)

Schnitz Pie

Makes 1 9" pie, or 8 slices
Prep Time: 30-40 minutes • Cooking Time: 45 minutes

3 cups dried apples

2¼ cups warm water

1 tsp. lemon extract

⅔ cup brown sugar

9" unbaked pie
crust, plus top crust

1. Soak apples in the warm water until plump and filled out.

2. Place apples and any remaining water in saucepan. Cover and cook until very soft.

3. Mash apples. Add lemon and sugar, stirring well.

4. Pour into unbaked pie crust.

5. Cover with top crust. Seal edges.

6. Bake at 425° for 15 minutes. Turn oven to 350° and continue baking for 30 more minutes.

Schnitz Pie is served each Sunday at the lunch following the church service. This pie can be made year-round; it doesn't depend on seasonal fruit. It can also be made in advance, an important advantage since the family hosting church in their home usually serves 75-100 people.

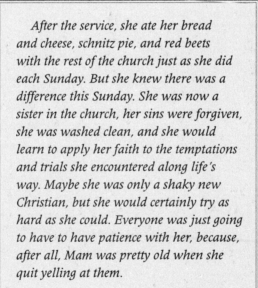

After the service, she ate her bread and cheese, schnitz pie, and red beets with the rest of the church just as she did each Sunday. But she knew there was a difference this Sunday. She was now a sister in the church, her sins were forgiven, she was washed clean, and she would learn to apply her faith to the temptations and trials she encountered along life's way. Maybe she was only a shaky new Christian, but she would certainly try as hard as she could. Everyone was just going to have to have patience with her, because, after all, Mam was pretty old when she quit yelling at them.

BIG DECISIONS

Chocolate Pie

Makes 2 9" pies, or 16 slices
Prep Time: 15 minutes • Chilling Time: 3-4 hours

1¼ cups sugar

2 tsp. vanilla

8-oz. pkg. cream cheese, softened

¾ cup milk

½ cup dry baking cocoa

16-oz. container frozen whipped topping, thawed (+ more, if you want to serve some on top of pie, too)

2 9" baked pie crusts (see page 215 for Pie Crust recipe)

1. In electric mixer bowl, combine sugar and vanilla.

2. Add cream cheese in chunks, beating thoroughly after each addition.

3. Stir in milk and baking cocoa.

4. Fold in whipped topping.

5. Divide mixture between 2 baked pie crusts.

6. Chill in fridge for 3-4 hours, so pie sets up and holds its shape when cut.

7. If you wish, top with dollops of whipped cream on each slice when serving.

Pie Crust

Makes 2 9" double-crust pies
Prep Time: 15 minutes for each double crust

4 cups flour

1 tsp. salt

1 tsp. baking powder

1 Tbsp. sugar

2 cups shortening (Crisco works well)

¼-⅓ cup water

1. In a large bowl, combine flour, salt, baking powder, and sugar.

2. Use a fork, or a pastry cutter, or 2 table knives to cut in shortening.

3. When mixture is crumbly and resembles small peas, add water, a few tablespoons at a time. Stir in water with a fork, using just enough water until the pastry forms a ball.

4. Using your hands, divide dough into 4 equal amounts.

5. Sprinkle work area with flour.

6. Roll out one ball of dough with a rolling pin.

7. Rolling away from yourself, make a circular pie crust about ⅛" thick and 2" bigger than the pie plate.

8. When the crust is the right size, loosely fold the dough in half and place into pie plate. Open up to fill plate. Press firmly in place with your fingers. *(continues on next page)*

Pie Crust

(continued)

9. Using a table knife, trim off the extra edges of the crust.

10. Fill the pie with desired pie filling.

11. To make a top crust, roll out a second ball of dough.

12. Rolling away from yourself, make a circular pie crust that is slightly thinner than the bottom crust and about 1" bigger than the pie plate.

13. Cut about 6 slits in this top dough crust, spacing the slits evenly, to allow steam to escape when the pie is baking.

14. Using a pastry brush or your fingers, moisten the edges of the bottom pie crust with cold water.

15. Place dough top carefully over pie filling.

16. Using your fingertips, press top and bottom edges together to seal.

17. Moving around the pie, pinch the edges into a V-shape to form fluting, or press firmly with tines of a fork.

18. Bake according to pie recipe.

19. Repeat this process with the other 2 balls of dough.

TO MAKE AN UNFILLED, BAKED PIE SHELL:

1. Follow steps 1-9 as directed above.

2. Moving around the pie, pinch the edges into a V-shape to form fluting, or press firmly with tines of a fork.

3. With a fork, prick the bottom and sides of crust.

4. Fill crust with pie weights to keep it from puffing up while baking.

5. Bake at 450° for 12-15 minutes, or until golden brown.

6. Cool and fill with filling of your choice, or continue to follow directions for your particular pie recipe.

Chocolate Whoopie Pies

Makes 4 dozen whoopie pies
Prep Time: 1 hour • Baking Time: 8-10 minutes

2 cups sugar
1 cup oil
2 eggs
4 cups flour
1 cup dry baking cocoa
1 tsp. salt
1 cup sour milk
2 tsp. vanilla
2 tsp. baking soda
1 cup hot water

1. Combine sugar, oil, and eggs in large mixing bowl. Beat until creamy.

2. Sift together flour, dry cocoa, and salt.

3. Add dry ingredients to creamed mixture alternately with sour milk.

4. Stir in vanilla.

5. In a separate bowl, whisk baking soda and hot water together until soda is dissolved.

6. Stir into batter until thoroughly mixed.

7. Drop by rounded teaspoonfuls onto well-greased baking sheets.

8. Bake at 400° for 8-10 minutes. To avoid dry whoopie pies, do not overbake.

9. Remove from sheets and allow to cool completely.

10. Spread filling (see recipe on page 220) on flat side of one cookie. Top with second cookie.

11. To store, wrap each whoopie pie in plastic wrap.

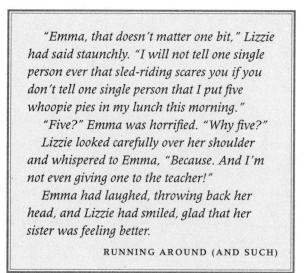

"Emma, that doesn't matter one bit," Lizzie had said staunchly. "I will not tell one single person ever that sled-riding scares you if you don't tell one single person that I put five whoopie pies in my lunch this morning."

"Five?" Emma was horrified. "Why five?"

Lizzie looked carefully over her shoulder and whispered to Emma, "Because. And I'm not even giving one to the teacher!"

Emma had laughed, throwing back her head, and Lizzie had smiled, glad that her sister was feeling better.

RUNNING AROUND (AND SUCH)

Whoopie Pie Filling

Makes 6 cups, enough for 2 dozen whoopie pies
Prep Time: 5 minutes

2 egg whites, beaten

4 cups confectioners sugar, *divided*

1 tsp. vanilla

1½ cups Crisco

1. Mix together egg whites, 2 cups sugar, and vanilla.

2. Beat in Crisco and remaining sugar.

3. Spread on flat side of whoopie pie "cookie." Top with second cookie. Be sure to use plenty of filling for each cookie.

She baked whoopie pies, wrapped them individually in plastic wrap, and kept eating them just about all day.

The thing about whoopie pies is that they stick to the plastic wrap in chocolatey layers, and when you pull the wrap away, the part underneath is so soft and good and so close to the creamy white frosting that you take one big bite after another, and before you know it, it's all gone and you want another one.

BIG DECISIONS

Pumpkin Whoopie Pies

Makes 2-3 dozen whoopie pies

Prep Time: 30 minutes • Baking Time: 10-15 minutes

2 cups brown sugar

1 cup oil

1½ cups canned pumpkin

3 cups all-purpose flour

1 tsp. baking powder

1 tsp. baking soda

1 tsp. cinnamon

½ tsp. ground ginger

1. In a large bowl, combine brown sugar, oil, and canned pumpkin until well mixed.

2. Stir in remaining ingredients, mixing well.

3. Drop by teaspoonfuls on well-greased baking sheets.

4. Bake at 375° for 10-15 minutes, or until toothpick inserted in center of cookies comes out clean.

5. Remove from cookie sheets and allow to cool.

6. Spread whoopie pie filling (see Filling recipe on page 220) on flat side of a cookie. Top with a second cookie, making a "sandwich."

7. To store, wrap each cookie in plastic wrap.

> *She unwrapped a pumpkin whoopie pie and took a huge, soft bite. The icing stuck to her cheek, and she wiped it away with her hand. Mmmm. Mam made the best whoopie pies.*
>
> RUNNING AROUND (AND SUCH)

Chocolate Chip Cookies

Makes 4 dozen cookies

Prep Time: 30 minutes • Baking Time: 8-10 minutes

3 cups brown sugar

1½ cups vegetable oil

4 eggs

3½-oz. box instant vanilla pudding

1 tsp. salt

2 tsp. vanilla extract

4½ cups all-purpose flour, *divided*

1½-2 cups chocolate chips

1. In large bowl, combine brown sugar, vegetable oil, and eggs. Stir until thoroughly combined.

2. Stir in pudding mix, salt, and vanilla extract, again until well combined.

3. Add flour 1 cup at a time, mixing well after each addition of flour.

4. Stir in chocolate chips.

5. Drop by teaspoonfuls onto greased cookie sheet.

6. Bake at 350° for 8-10 minutes, or until cookies are golden brown around the edges.

TIP:

Do not overbake these very soft cookies.

Hot chocolate tasted even better with a chocolate chip cookie to dip into it. Chocolate chip cookies were funny things, though. They were almost a staple in an Amish child's lunchbox. All the mothers made chocolate chip cookies. They made molasses cookies and whoopie pies and snickerdoodles and raisin cookies, too, but the most popular was always chocolate chip.

Aunt Becca's chocolate chip cookies were the best, hands down, Lizzie thought. They were firm and chewy and a tiny bit overbaked. If you broke one in half, you could hold it in the hot chocolate for a long time, and then lift it to your mouth with style and grace.

Lizzie never did, though. She just wolfed them down, dripping hot chocolate on the front of her coat. She was dismayed to find that she had already eaten four cookies and probably could have eaten four more.

But chocolate chip cookies were as unpredictable as the weather. Each mother had a different recipe. Some cookies were hard as a rock, but they were the best to dip in hot chocolate.

Others were high and dry and, the minute they hit that creamy liquid, dissolved into a warm mushy mess. You couldn't get them to your open mouth fast enough before they disintegrated and landed in the bottom of the cup. If you were lucky, a few chocolate chips floated to the top, and you could at least rescue them.

BIG DECISIONS

Peanut Butter Chocolate Chip Cookies

Makes 7-8 dozen cookies

Prep Time: 30 minutes • Baking Time: 8-10 minutes

2 cups flour

1 tsp. baking soda

½ tsp. salt

1 cup granulated sugar

1 cup brown sugar

1 cup shortening,
or butter (2 sticks),
softened

2 eggs

1 tsp. vanilla

1 cup creamy peanut
butter

1 cup chocolate chips

1 cup chopped,
unsalted peanuts,
optional

1. Sift flour, baking soda, and salt together in medium-sized bowl. Set aside.

2. In large mixing bowl, cream together sugars and shortening.

3. Add eggs and vanilla to creamed mixture. Beat until fluffy.

4. Stir in peanut butter.

5. Add sifted ingredients and mix well.

6. Stir in chocolate chips and peanuts if you wish.

7. Drop by teaspoonfuls onto well-greased cookie sheets.

8. Bake at 350° for 8-10 minutes.

They ate thick roast beef sandwiches
with slabs of Swiss cheese and lettuce from
Rebecca's garden. Rebecca had thought
to pack small Tupperware containers of
mayonnaise and mustard which made the
sandwiches taste so good.

Lizzie had packed a bag with potato
chips, homemade dill pickles, peanut butter
chocolate chip cookies, and large red apples,
polished until they looked like a picture in a
storybook.

The whole picnic lunch was so delicious,
the cookies melting in Lizzie's mouth and
then washed down with that wonderful ice-
cold meadow tea.

WHEN STRAWBERRIES BLOOM

Chocolate Chip Cookie Bars

Makes 24 bars

Prep Time: 20 minutes • *Baking Time: 25 minutes*

1 stick + 2⅔ Tbsp. (⅔ cup)
butter, softened

1½ cups brown sugar

½ cup granulated sugar

3 eggs

1 tsp. vanilla

2 cups flour

1 tsp. baking powder

½ tsp. salt

1 cup chocolate chips

½ cup chopped pecans,
optional

1. In large bowl, cream together butter and sugars.

2. Beat in eggs and vanilla.

3. Stir in flour, baking powder, and salt.

4. Add chocolate chips and nuts if you wish.

5. Spread in well-greased 12" × 15" jelly-roll pan.

6. Bake at 350° for 25 minutes.

7. When bars have cooled, cut with a plastic knife (which makes smoother edges for the bars than a metal knife).

They all took turns holding Laura, while KatieAnn and Susan entertained the other children with Mary's help. Everyone chattered and exclaimed and talked all at once, and no one truly listened much to what other persons were saying. After the initial frenzy of seeing the baby and saying the most important things had died down, they had coffee around the kitchen table, savoring the chocolate chip bars, and talking at a much more normal volume and speed.

BIG DECISIONS

Butterscotch Nut Cookies

Makes about 7 dozen cookies
Prep Time: 20 minutes
Chilling Time: 2-3 hours • *Baking Time: 8-10 minutes*

2 cups brown sugar

2 eggs

2 sticks (1 cup) butter, softened

1 tsp. vanilla

3½ cups flour

1 tsp. baking soda

1 tsp. cream of tartar

1 cup chopped walnuts *or* pecans

1. In large mixer bowl, combine brown sugar, eggs, and butter.

2. Add vanilla and beat until thoroughly combined.

3. Stir in flour, baking soda, cream of tartar, and nuts until well blended.

4. Shape dough into logs about 2" around. (If dough is too soft to handle, chill in fridge for 1 hour, and then try again.)

5. Wrap each log in plastic wrap. Chill for at least 2 hours.

6. Unwrap dough and slice into ¼"-thick pieces.

7. Lay slices flat on well-greased cookie sheet. Allow about 1" between slices.

8. Bake at 350° for 8-10 minutes.

Lizzie's intensive sewing lessons continued during the week after her birthday. One morning, after the breakfast dishes were done, Lizzie and Emma spread out dress fabric on the kitchen table while Mam baked cookies.

"It's not straight," Lizzie wailed, as she started to cut into the fabric.

"Hold your scissors upside down, Lizzie. You're left-handed."

"Ow! Ouch. That doesn't work either. It cuts right into the soft part of my thumb."

RUNNING AROUND
(AND SUCH)

Molasses Cookies

Makes 4 dozen cookies

Prep Time: 30-40 minutes • Baking Time: 10-12 minutes

1½ cups vegetable oil

2 cups brown sugar

2 eggs

¾ cup molasses (Brer Rabbit is best!)

4 tsp. baking soda

½ tsp. salt

1 tsp. ground ginger

2 tsp. ground cinnamon

5 cups all-purpose flour, *divided*

1 cup granulated sugar

1. In large bowl, combine oil, brown sugar, and eggs, mixing well.

2. Stir in molasses until well blended.

3. Add baking soda, salt, ginger, and cinnamon, mixing well.

4. Add flour one cup at a time, mixing thoroughly after each addition of flour. The dough will be stiff.

5. Place granulated sugar into a shallow bowl or plate.

6. Using a teaspoon, scoop out dough and roll into a small ball. Roll the unbaked cookie in granulated sugar.

7. Place cookies on well-greased cookie sheets.

8. Flatten slightly with the back of a spoon before baking.

9. Bake at 350° for 10-12 minutes.

Lizzie shared Mam's homemade cupcakes filled with lovely white frosting or her big, round molasses cookies sprinkled with sugar.

They covered many subjects as they ate. Dora even talked about getting married, although shyly and a bit wistfully. Lizzie felt so sorry for her, it actually hurt. Lizzie admitted that she couldn't wait to turn 16 and start dating. But who would ask her?

RUNNING AROUND
(AND SUCH)

Grandpa Cookies

Makes 10 dozen cookies

Prep Time: 30 minutes • *Baking Time: 12-15 minutes*

2 sticks (½ lb.)
butter, softened

3 cups brown sugar

5 eggs

1 cup sour cream

4¾ cups flour

1 Tbsp. baking soda

1 Tbsp. baking
powder

1. Cream butter and sugar in large bowl.

2. Add eggs and sour cream. Beat well.

3. Add remaining ingredients and stir to combine.

4. Drop by teaspoonfuls onto well-greased cookie sheets.

5. Bake at 375° for 12-15 minutes.

6. Frost with Caramel Frosting (see recipe on page 239) or Creamy Jelly Roll Topping (see recipe on page 245).

Sand Tarts

Makes 4-5 dozen cookies
Prep Time: 30-45 minutes
Chilling Time: 6-8 hours, or overnight • Baking Time: 8-10 minutes

2 sticks butter
(½ pound),
softened

3 cups
brown sugar

4 eggs, *divided*

1 tsp. vanilla

4 cups
all-purpose flour

1 tsp.
cream of tartar

1 tsp. baking soda

sugar, cinnamon,
and/or sprinkles
for topping

1. In large bowl, cream butter and sugar together.

2. Add 3 eggs and vanilla. Reserve 1 egg for topping.

3. Stir in flour, cream of tartar, and baking soda.

4. Roll dough into ball and wrap in plastic wrap. Chill 6-8 hours, or overnight.

5. Roll out chilled dough so that it is ¼" thick.

6. Using cookie cutters, cut out dough. Place on greased baking sheets, about 1" apart.

7. In a small bowl, beat 1 egg. Using a pastry brush, brush the tops of the cookies with the beaten egg.

8. Sprinkle cookies with sugar, cinnamon, and/or sprinkles.

9. Bake at 350° for 8-10 minutes.

Chocolate Cake

Makes 9 × 13 pan
Prep Time: 15 minutes • Baking Time: 20-30 minutes

¾ cup oil

2 cups granulated sugar

3 eggs

2½ cups flour

¾ cup dry baking cocoa

2 tsp. baking powder

2 tsp. baking soda

1 cup sour milk, *or* buttermilk

1 cup liquid hot coffee

1. In medium bowl, mix together oil, sugar, and eggs.

2. In separate bowl, sift together flour, dry baking cocoa, baking powder, and baking soda.

3. Add flour mixture alternately with milk to sugar mixture. Beat well after each addition.

4. Stir in hot coffee. Batter will be lumpy.

5. Pour cake batter into well-greased 9" × 13" cake pan, or 2 round cake pans.

6. Bake at 350° for 20-30 minutes, or until a toothpick inserted in center of cake comes out clean.

7. When cake is cool, frost with your favorite frosting.

Dear, bossy, big sister Emma. And now Emma had turned 16. Tonight the family gathered around the dining room table to celebrate Emma's big birthday. Each person had a lovely glass dish filled with chocolate cake and vanilla ice cream while Emma opened her gifts. The birthday cake had two layers covered with vanilla frosting—everyone's favorite—and they enjoyed every last morsel of it with spoonfuls of creamy vanilla ice cream.

RUNNING AROUND
(AND SUCH)

Christmas Cake

Makes 1 two-layer cake
Prep Time: 20 minutes
Baking Time: 30-35 minutes • Cooling Time: 1 hour

1½ sticks (¾ cup) butter, softened

2 cups granulated sugar

4 eggs, separated

3 cups flour

4 tsp. baking powder

1 cup milk

¾ cup chopped walnuts, *or* pecans, *divided*

1. Cream butter and sugar together until well blended.

2. Separate eggs. Add egg yolks to creamed mixture. Beat well. (Reserve egg whites in separate bowl.)

3. Stir flour and baking powder together in bowl.

4. Add milk alternately with flour and baking powder to creamed mixture, stirring well after each addition.

5. Stir in ½ cup chopped nuts.

6. Beat egg whites until frothy. Fold into batter.

7. Pour batter into 2 lightly greased 9" round cake pans.

8. Bake at 350° for 30-35 minutes, or until toothpick inserted in centers comes out clean.

9. Cool cakes to room temperature.

10. Frost with Caramel Frosting (see page 239).

11. Sprinkle top with reserved nuts.

> *There was hardly an end to the rich desserts and drinks Mam would cook and bake for weeks before Christmas. She made butterscotch pie, chocolate pie, sand tarts, Grandpa cookies, Christmas layer salad, banana pudding, and Christmas cake. Mam mixed ginger ale with grape juice, or she bought soda—Mountain Dew, Pepsi, or root beer—and vanilla ice cream to make root beer floats. Which, Lizzie discovered as a child, you should never eat with olives.*
>
> RUNNING AROUND (AND SUCH)

Chocolate Cupcakes

Makes 1 dozen cupcakes
Prep Time: 20 minutes • Baking Time: 10-15 minutes

1 cup sugar
1 egg
½ cup vegetable oil
1 cup dry baking cocoa
1½ cups flour
½ cup sour milk
1 tsp. baking soda
1 tsp. vanilla
½ cup hot water

1. Combine sugar, egg, and oil in large bowl. Mix well.

2. Add remaining ingredients, following the order listed. Beat well.

3. Line muffin pans with cupcake liners. Fill each liner ½ to ⅔ full.

4. Bake at 350° for 10-15 minutes, or until toothpick inserted in centers of cupcakes comes out clean.

5. Remove from pan and allow to cool before frosting.

TIP:

Any cake recipe can be converted to cupcakes. Just bake in muffin tins instead of cake pans and bake for 10-15 minutes.

Caramel Frosting

Makes 3-4 cups frosting
Prep Time: 5 minutes
Cooking Time: 5-10 minutes • Cooling Time: 1-2 hours

1½ cups brown sugar

1½ sticks (¾ cup) butter, cut into chunks

⅓ cup milk

1 tsp. vanilla

3-4 cups confectioners sugar

1. In medium saucepan, combine brown sugar and butter. Heat until boiling, stirring continually. Allow to boil for 1 minute, stirring the whole time.

2. Add milk. Bring to boiling point again, stirring constantly.

3. Allow to cool to room temperature.

4. Stir in vanilla.

5. Stir in confectioners sugar until the icing is spreadable, but not runny.

6. Spread on Christmas Cake (page 236), Cupcakes (page 238), or Grandpa Cookies (page 232).

> *The wind whistled softly around the eaves of the farmhouse as Mam frosted cupcakes and Dat sipped his coffee. It was a cozy, secure feeling, being there in the kitchen with Dat and Mam, both of them smiling contentedly.*
>
> RUNNING AROUND (AND SUCH)

Seven-Minute Frosting

For 1 cake

Prep Time: 15 minutes • Cooking Time: 7 minutes

2 egg whites
1½ cups sugar
⅓ cup cold water
1 Tbsp. light corn syrup
1 tsp. vanilla
¼ tsp. cream of tartar
⅛ tsp. salt

1. Separate eggs into 2 bowls: 1 for the whites; 1 for the yolks. Place whites in medium saucepan. (Save yolks for another use.)

2. Combine all other ingredients with egg whites in saucepan.

3. Bring mixture to a boil and allow to cook for 7 minutes.

4. With a mixer or egg beater, beat until light and fluffy.

5. Spread on cake and serve.

Suddenly Mam came bustling out to the kitchen, her cheeks flushed, excitement making her eyes snap. Dat followed her, a big silly grin on his face as he sat at the table. Jason slid in beside Mandy, looking at Lizzie and back again to Mandy.

"Bet you wish you had a boyfriend," he teased.

Dat laughed, slapping the table with his open palm. "Now, Jase!" he said.

Mam opened the refrigerator door, checking to see if her seven-minute frosting had cooled properly. She tasted it, nodded her head, and got the bowl out of the refrigerator so she could ice the big round chocolate cupcakes.

"They might be hungry when they come home," Mam said softly.

RUNNING AROUND (AND SUCH)

Jelly Roll

4 eggs at room temperature

¼ tsp. salt

¾ tsp. baking powder

¾ cup granulated sugar

¾ cup cake flour

1 tsp. vanilla

1. Combine eggs, salt, and baking powder. Beat with mixer, gradually adding sugar. Mixture will be light in color and slightly thickened.

2. Add cake flour and vanilla.

3. Line a 10" × 15" baking pan with waxed paper. Grease waxed paper and sprinkle a little flour on top.

4. Pour batter onto waxed paper in pan.

5. Bake at 400° for 6-8 minutes, or until toothpick inserted in center comes out clean.

6. Sprinkle powdered sugar onto a tea towel or a long stretch of waxed paper.

7. When jelly roll is finished baking, flip onto sugared tea towel or waxed paper.

8. Starting at the narrow end of the jelly roll, gently roll the tea towel and jelly roll together into a log shape.

9. Allow to cool completely.

10. When cooled, unroll the jelly roll and spread with filling (see page 244).

11. Roll up the jelly roll with filling inside.

12. To serve, place on platter or tray with the beginning of the roll facing down. Cut into 1"- 2"-thick slices.

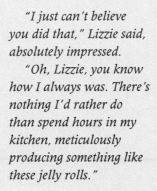

"I just can't believe you did that," Lizzie said, absolutely impressed.
"Oh, Lizzie, you know how I always was. There's nothing I'd rather do than spend hours in my kitchen, meticulously producing something like these jelly rolls."

RUNNING AROUND
(AND SUCH)

Jelly Roll Filling

Makes enough filling for 1 jelly roll
Prep Time: 15 minutes
Cooking Time: approximately 5 minutes • Cooling Time: 1 hour

4 Tbsp. flour

¼ cup brown sugar

¼ tsp. salt

⅔ cup hot water

½ stick (4 Tbsp.) butter, cut into chunks

1½ tsp. vanilla

food coloring, *optional*

1. In a small saucepan, combine flour, sugar, and salt.

2. Add water, stirring constantly, and heat until the mixture becomes smooth and thickens.

3. Remove from heat. Stir in butter and vanilla until butter melts.

4. If you wish, stir in food coloring.

5. Allow to cool before spreading on cooled jelly roll.

Mandy oohed and aahed about the lemon jelly roll Emma held, while Lizzie said the chocolate one looked like a picture in a magazine. It did. Emma had made two perfect cake rolls. The lemon one was piped full of a light lemon filling that smelled so delicious Lizzie's mouth watered. The other cake was a rich chocolate filled with creamy vanilla frosting. Emma had dusted both with confectioners sugar. The cakes were perfectly round without a crack or a burnt edge in sight.

RUNNING AROUND (AND SUCH)

Creamy Jelly Roll Topping

Makes enough topping for 1 jelly roll
Prep Time: 10 minutes

8-oz. pkg. cream cheese, softened to room temperature

9-oz. pkg. frozen whipped topping, thawed

2 cups confectioners sugar

1. In a good-sized bowl, beat cream cheese until creamy.

2. Fold in whipped topping.

3. Gently stir in confectioners sugar, mixing well.

4. Spread mixture on cooled jelly roll before slicing it.

NOTE:

This topping can also be used as frosting for cupcakes.

Banana Pudding

Makes 25-30 servings
Prep Time: 20 minutes

3 3.4-oz. pkgs. instant vanilla pudding

5 cups milk

2 8-oz. boxes vanilla wafers, *divided*

12-15 ripe bananas, sliced, *divided*

16-oz. container frozen whipped topping, thawed

1. Make vanilla pudding by following directions on the box, using the 5 cups milk.

2. In a very large bowl, or in two large bowls, make a layer of half the wafers, then a layer of half the sliced bananas, and a layer of half the pudding.

3. Repeat layers.

4. Top with a layer of whipped topping.

5. Cover and refrigerate until ready to serve.

TIPS:

1. Substitute crushed graham crackers instead of vanilla wafers if you wish.

2. This is enough Pudding for a big party. You can make ⅓ of this recipe and serve 8-10 people.

Mandy ran up to the porch swing,
backed up, and said, "Slide over."

The peaceful swinging resumed
as Mandy finished her cake and
pudding.

"Emma, you're going to miss us
when you move!" Mandy said.

"You'll come visit me, I hope."

"Yes."

"But you know very well how I
always was, Mandy. This is what I
wanted since I was a little girl, not
much older than eight years old.
To be alone in my old farmhouse,
cooking and cleaning, baking good
things and washing my very own
dishes—it's just too good to be true."

WHEN STRAWBERRIES BLOOM

Vanilla Cornstarch Pudding

Makes 15-20 servings
Prep Time: 10 minutes • Cooking Time: 15 minutes
Chilling Time: 3-4 hours, or overnight

2 quarts milk
1½ cups sugar
3 heaping Tbsp. cornstarch
5 eggs
1 tsp. vanilla
8-oz., *or* **16-oz., pkg. frozen whipped topping, thawed**

1. In large saucepan, heat milk until just to the boiling point, but do not boil.

2. In a bowl, beat sugar, cornstarch, and eggs together until foamy.

3. Add one cup of hot milk into egg mixture, stirring constantly until well mixed.

4. Slowly pour all of egg mixture into hot milk.

5. Stirring constantly, cook over low heat until thickened.

6. Remove from heat and stir in vanilla.

7. Cool completely, 3-4 hours, or overnight.

8. Stir desired amount of whipped topping into chilled pudding just before serving.

TIP:

You can cut the ingredients of this large recipe in half and still have good results.

> Lizzie sat tightly against Emma, and Mandy wiggled in on the other side. Lizzie peered into her dish. Chocolate cake and vanilla pudding. Mmmm!
> "One bite!" Mandy said, knowing Lizzie's appetite. "A big one."
> Mandy cut off a huge piece of cake, loaded it with vanilla pudding, held it in front of Lizzie's face.
> "Open wide!"
> Lizzie did, and her mouth was promptly filled with a huge bite of cake, the whole spoon, and vanilla pudding squishing everywhere. Lizzie made funny noises, and Mandy threw back her head, howling with glee, as Lizzie struggled to keep everything in her mouth. After she had swallowed, Mandy jumped up, knowing from experience she would catch it from Lizzie.
>
> RUNNING AROUND (AND SUCH)

Date Pudding

Makes 20 servings
Prep Time: 30-45 minutes • Baking Time: 30-35 minutes
Cooling Time: 2-3 hours

1 cup chopped dates
1 tsp. baking soda
1 Tbsp. butter, softened
1 cup boiling water
2 eggs
1 cup flour
1 cup sugar
1 tsp. vanilla
¾ cup nuts, chopped

Sauce:
2 cups water
1 cup brown sugar
1 stick (8 Tbsp.) butter
½ cup flour
2-3 Tbsp. water

16-oz. pkg. frozen whipped topping, thawed

1. In a large bowl, combine dates, baking soda, and butter.

2. Bring water to a boil.

3. Cover date mixture with boiling water. Mix well and let cool.

4. When dates are cool, add eggs, flour, sugar, vanilla, and chopped nuts. Stir well.

5. Pour mixture into well-greased 9" × 13" baking pan.

6. Bake at 325° for 30-35 minutes, or until a toothpick inserted in center comes out clean.

7. Allow to cool. Then cut pudding into 1" squares.

8. To make sauce, pour 2 cups water, brown sugar, and butter into medium saucepan. Bring to a boil, stirring frequently.

9. In a small bowl, blend flour with 2-3 Tbsp. of water until smooth.

10. Stir flour mixture into hot syrup. Stir constantly and bring again to a boil.

11. Remove from heat and cool completely.

12. To serve, layer ⅓ pudding squares on bottom of large bowl. Add ⅓ of sauce and ⅓ of whipped topping.

13. Repeat two more times until bowl is filled with three layers.

14. Cover. Chill in fridge until ready to serve.

Aunt Vera made mountains of date pudding at home in Ohio, bringing it all the way to Pennsylvania with buckets of whipped topping for the big day. Date pudding was Lizzie's favorite dessert, ever since she had first tasted it as a little girl in Ohio. It was a soft, moist cake baked with dates and nuts, then cut into tiny squares and layered with a caramel sauce and whipped topping. It was rich and creamy with a nutty texture that was simply delicious. They served it on every table throughout the house, with small squares of red and green Jell-O on top, because their wedding was so close to Christmas.

BIG DECISIONS

Doughnuts

Makes 25-40 doughnuts

Prep Time: 45 minutes • *Rising Time: 2-3 hours*
Frying Time: 5-10 minutes • *Cooling Time: 20 minutes*

¾ Tbsp. yeast

½ cup warm water (110-115°)

1 cup milk

¼ cup granulated sugar

1 egg

½ cup mashed potatoes

¼ cup vegetable oil

¼ tsp. salt

4 cups flour

5-6 pounds solid vegetable shortening

Glaze:

4 cups confectioners sugar

6 Tbsp. heavy whipping cream

2 Tbsp. cornstarch

1 tsp. vanilla

water to thin glaze

1. Dissolve yeast in warm water and set aside.

2. In large saucepan, heat milk and sugar just until hot. Do not boil.

3. In separate bowl, beat egg.

4. Stir beaten egg, mashed potatoes, and vegetable oil into milk.

5. Add yeast mixture to milk mixture and stir well.

6. Add salt and flour. Beat well until dough is sticky.

7. Cover dough with plastic wrap or tea towel. Let rise until double in size, approximately 1-2 hours.

8. Sprinkle counter or tabletop liberally with flour to prevent dough from sticking. Line cookie sheets with waxed paper and sprinkle with flour.

9. Roll out dough on work space until it is approximately ¼" thick.

10. With a doughnut cutter, or any circle-shaped cutter, cut out doughnuts.

11. Place doughnuts on prepared cookie sheets. Cover. Allow them to rise until doubled in size, approximately 1 hour.

12. Melt shortening over medium heat until it reaches a temperature of 350-375°.

13. Fry 3 or 4 doughnuts at a time, just until golden brown on top. Flip and brown on second side, watching carefully and removing quickly.

14. Using a colander, drain the shortening off the doughnuts.

15. Cool completely before glazing.

16. To make the glaze, mix confectioners sugar, heavy whipping cream, cornstarch, and vanilla in a medium bowl. Add water until the glaze is the desired consistency.

17. To glaze the doughnuts, dip the doughnuts into the glaze, flipping them over so that glaze covers both sides.

18. Using a dinner fork or fingers, remove the doughnut and allow excess glaze to drip off.

> *After the celery was all washed and sorted, the whole group took a coffee break and snacked on all kinds of cookies and doughnuts.*
> WHEN STRAWBERRIES BLOOM

Cream Sticks

Makes about 2½ dozen sticks

Prep Time: 20-30 minutes • Rising Time: 1¼-2½ hours
Frying Time: a few minutes per batch

1 cup milk

2 Tbsp. yeast

1 cup warm water
(110-115°)

½ cup vegetable
shortening

⅔ cup sugar

2 eggs, beaten

1 tsp. salt

6 cups flour, *divided*

vegetable oil for
deep frying

1. Heat milk until almost boiling. Remove from heat and allow to cool.

2. In a small bowl, dissolve yeast in warm water.

3. In a large bowl, combine shortening, sugar, eggs, and salt.

4. Add milk and yeast mixture to shortening mixture.

5. Slowly add flour, 2-3 cups at a time. Mix in until dough is soft.

6. Cover and let rise until dough has doubled in size, approximately 1-2 hours.

7. Sprinkle flour on work area. Roll out dough on work area until ¼"– ½" thick.

8. Cut dough into rectangles 4" × 1" in size. Place on baking sheets about 1" apart.

9. Cover and let rise until dough is almost double in size, approximately 15-30 minutes.

10. To fry, heat vegetable oil in large saucepan to 375°.

11. Carefully drop 3 or 4 cream sticks at a time into hot oil and fry until golden brown, turning once.

12. Remove from oil and cool.

Of course, Mam made cream sticks for coffee break in the morning. They were homemade doughnuts, with the dough cut in rectangles, fried in deep fat, a slit cut along each top, and filled with creamy vanilla frosting. Golden caramel icing was spread on top, resulting in achingly sweet, oblong, filled doughnuts, which in Emma's words were so good it wasn't even right.

When the men finished eating, they paid Mam warm compliments. She dipped her head, her cheeks flushed, basking in the words of praise. Dat acted so conceited when someone praised Mam's cooking that the girls hid their smiles behind their hands. He wasn't very tall, but he grew a few inches whenever that happened, Emma would say.

WHEN STRAWBERRIES BLOOM

Filling for Cream Sticks

Makes cream for 2½ dozen sticks
Prep Time: 15-20 minutes

3 tsp. flour
1 cup milk
1 cup vegetable shortening
1 cup sugar
1 Tbsp. vanilla
2½ cups confectioners sugar

1. In small saucepan, combine flour and milk until it forms a smooth paste.

2. Bring to a boil, stirring constantly.

3. Remove from heat and cool.

4. In medium electric mixer bowl, beat together shortening, sugar, and vanilla.

5. Add flour and milk mixture. Stir well.

6. Beat in confectioners sugar.

7. Cut slits in the cooled cream sticks to fill with filling. Use a cookie press or cake decorating kit to fill cream sticks.

*Once, after Mam had made
cream sticks, Lizzie ate four.
Cream sticks were homemade
doughnuts, but instead of being
round with a hole in the middle,
they were cut in an oblong shape.
After they were deep-fried, Mam
cut a long slit in each of their
tops, filled them with creamy
vanilla icing, and then put
golden caramel frosting on the
tops. They were the very best
thing in the world of desserts,
but Mam didn't make them very
often because they were so much
work, with two different kinds of
icing and all.*

RUNNING AROUND
(AND SUCH)

Topping for Cream Sticks

Makes enough topping for 2½ dozen sticks
Prep Time: 10 minutes • Cooling Time: 1 hour

½ stick (4 Tbsp.)
butter

1 cup brown sugar

⅓ cup milk

½ cup vegetable
shortening

2 cups
confectioners
sugar

1. In medium saucepan, melt butter.

2. Add brown sugar and milk.

3. Stirring frequently, bring mixture to a boil.

4. Remove from heat and cool.

5. When mixture is cool, stir in shortening.

6. When smooth, stir in confectioners sugar. Beat until smooth.

7. Spread on top of filled cream sticks.

Beverages

Lemonade

Makes 1 gallon

Prep Time: 10 minutes • Standing Time: 10 minutes

3 lemons, sliced
very thin

2 cups sugar

1 gallon water

1. Using a potato masher, pound sugar into pulp of lemon slices. Let stand 10 minutes.

2. Fish out the lemon slices and squeeze them, extracting as much juice as possible. Discard rinds.

3. Add water to sugar-pulp and ice to taste.

*The happiness she felt from having
completed two weeks in Dunnville spread
its warm glow through her heart for quite
a while. She was so glad to be at home and
so happy to sleep with Mandy in their bed.
They giggled and read books by the light
of the kerosene lamp, which they perched
precariously over their mattress. Sometimes
they tiptoed to the kitchen for bologna and
cheese sandwiches, along with some lemonade,
taking the goodies back to their room for a
late-night picnic on the floor.*

RUNNING AROUND (AND SUCH)

*Then she went to the house to make a
pitcher of lemonade. The sun was beginning
its descent, dipping below the mountain, and
a small flock of blackbirds fussed and twittered
their way across the evening sky, the way
blackbirds did when they started to sense the
end of summer.*

*Stephen watched their flight, drank his
lemonade, and said nothing. Lizzie clasped
her hands around her knees, pulling her skirt
down till only her bare toes were visible, and
sighed happily.*

BIG DECISIONS

Meadow Tea to Drink Right Away

Makes 1½ gallons
Prep Time: 10 minutes • Steeping Time: 10-15 minutes

2 cups fresh tea leaves,
peppermint, spearmint,
or whatever is growing in
your garden

1½ gallons water

sugar to taste

1. Rinse tea leaves in cold water.

2. Bring water to a boil.

3. Submerge tea leaves in boiling water and turn off burner.

4. Allow to steep 10-15 minutes.

5. Remove all tea leaves. Squeeze, without burning your hands, to extract all juice.

6. Add sugar to taste while tea is hot. Stir to dissolve.

7. Chill tea immediately. Serve with ice.

Rebecca poured ice-cold meadow tea into plastic cups, which Lizzie drank gratefully. As soon as her cup was empty, she asked for more. In all the world, there is nothing more refreshing than meadow tea on a hot day, Lizzie thought.

WHEN
STRAWBERRIES
BLOOM

Meadow Tea Concentrate to Freeze

Makes 6 quarts concentrate
Prep Time: 5 minutes • Cooking Time: 5 minutes
Steeping Time: 6-7 hours, or overnight

24 cups water

6-8 cups sugar

12 cups fresh
tea leaves

1. In large pot, boil water and sugar for 5 minutes.

2. Add tea leaves. Submerge in hot water. Allow to steep 6-7 hours or overnight.

3. Strain tea.

4. Pour into containers and freeze.

5. To make tea, combine 3 parts water to 1 part tea.

> *In the kitchen, the mood was dispelled, the atmosphere lighter, and Stephen bantered lightheartedly, as usual, while they ate the Christmas cookies and drank hot peppermint tea.*
>
> WHEN STRAWBERRIES BLOOM

Quick Homemade Root Beer

Makes 1 gallon
Prep Time: 10 minutes • Steeping Time: 4 hours
Chilling Time: 8 hours, or overnight

2 cups sugar

4 tsp. root beer extract

¾ tsp. yeast

1 gallon lukewarm water, *divided*

1. In small bowl, mix together sugar, root beer extract, and yeast.

2. Pour into 1 gallon jug.

3. Add ½ gallon lukewarm water.

4. Shake or stir until sugar is dissolved.

5. Add remaining ½ gallon of lukewarm water.

6. Cap tightly and set in sun 4 hours.

7. Chill overnight.

8. Serve the next day.

TIP:

A yummy way to enjoy root beer: Put one or two scoops of vanilla ice cream in the bottom of a glass. Pour root beer over ice cream. Stir and enjoy.

> *Mam mixed ginger ale with grape juice, or she bought soda—Mountain Dew, Pepsi, or root beer— and vanilla ice cream to make root beer floats. Which, Lizzie discovered as a child, you should never eat with olives.*
>
> WHEN STRAWBERRIES BLOOM

French Chocolate

Makes 16-18 servings
Prep Time: 20 minutes

¾ cup chocolate chips
½ cup light corn syrup
⅓ cup water
1 tsp. vanilla
1 pint whipping cream
2 quarts milk

1. In a medium saucepan, combine chocolate chips, corn syrup, and water. Heat over low heat until chips melt, stirring frequently.

2. Add vanilla and allow to cool.

3. In separate bowl, beat cream until thick.

4. Adding a small portion at a time, slowly beat in chocolate mixture.

5. Place in fridge until ready to use.

6. Before serving, heat milk to almost boiling.

7. Fill favorite mug half-full of creamy chocolate mixture.

8. Fill to the top with hot milk.

9. Stir and serve.

> *Thermoses of hot chocolate and a large container for water were set on the sleds, cushioned with old quilts. A toboggan, for the little ones, was carefully lined with buggy robes.*
>
> BIG DECISIONS

Hot Chocolate Mix

Prep Time: 5 minutes

8-quart pkg. powdered milk

16-oz. container Nestle Nesquik

1 pint non-dairy coffee creamer

1 pound (2 cups) confectioners sugar

1 bag mini-marshmallows, *optional*

1. Mix together all ingredients.

2. Store in an airtight container.

3. To make one cup of hot chocolate, add boiling water to ⅓ cup of mix.

She decided to drink a cup of hot chocolate before lacing up her skates. There was just something about a steaming cup of hot chocolate on a cold winter day, Lizzie thought, that made your heart so cozy you could hardly stand it. It felt like the softest cashmere scarf around your stomach, soothing it and warming your whole body until you felt fluffy all over.
BIG DECISIONS

Mam's Hot Chocolate

Makes 4 servings

Prep Time: 5 minutes • Cooking Time: 10 minutes

¼ cup water

1 Tbsp. powdered baking cocoa

3 Tbsp. sugar

4 cups milk

1. Pour water, baking cocoa, and sugar into medium saucepan. Boil for 2 minutes.

2. In a separate saucepan, heat milk just to boiling point.

3. Add chocolate mixture to warm milk and stir.

Mam smiled at Lizzie as she came into the kitchen. "All done?" she asked. "Did the wash freeze as fast as you hung it out?"

"Not really," Lizzie answered. "Mmm, these look good. May I make hot chocolate?"

"Go ahead," Mam said, turning to flip more freshly baked cookies expertly.

RUNNING AROUND (AND SUCH)

Canning

Recipes

Canning Tips for Pickles

1. First, wash the jars you'll be using.

2. Place upside down until completely dry.

3. Have new lids and clean jar rings ready. Rings can be used over and over.

4. Slice cucumbers into ½"-thick slices. Put into jars. Pour prepared juice or brine over sliced cucumbers, allowing 1" of headspace.

5. Always wipe rims of jars with a clean, wet, dishcloth before putting on lids and rings. Jars will not seal if juice is on the rim.

6. Place water in canner and bring to a boil.

7. Carefully place jars into canner of boiling water. Water should reach the bottoms of the jar rings, but never go over the lids.

8. Make sure water is boiling before timing the cooking.

9. Most pickles need to be cooked 10 minutes after coming to a boil.

10. After jars have boiled for 10 minutes, turn burner off.

11. Using a jar lifter, remove jars from hot water.

12. Keeping rings on jars, let rest for 24 hours.

13. After 24 hours, remove rings and make sure all lids have sealed. An unsealed jar can be refrigerated for several days. Discard contents after that.

14. Move sealed jars into a cool, dark place to store. Basements are ideal, but a pantry or cupboards work as well.

15. Home-canned foods are best used within 1 year. They are safe to use after 1 year, but they are not quite as flavorful.

Bread and Butter Pickles

Makes 4 quarts
Prep Time: 1-2 hours • Standing Time: 3 hours
Cooking Time: 10 minutes • Standing Time: 24 hours

1 gallon cucumbers
3 small onions
2 green bell peppers
½ cup salt
water

Brine:
5 cups sugar
1½ tsp. turmeric
2 Tbsp. mustard seed
3 cups vinegar
1 cup water

1. Without peeling cucumbers, slice thinly into large crock or clean bucket.

2. Slice onions and peppers thinly.

3. Add to cucumbers.

4. Sprinkle with salt.

5. Cover with cold water and let stand 3 hours.

6. After 3 hours, drain and rinse cucumbers.

7. Place cucumbers in jars.

8. Combine brine ingredients in large stockpot.

9. Boil 3-5 minutes.

10. Pour brine over cucumbers in jars, allowing 1" of headspace in each jar.

11. Follow "Canning Tips for Pickles" instructions on page 270, beginning with Step 5.

> *They filled little pint jars with pickles, red beets, grape jelly, and applesauce. They put peaches and pears in quart jars. Mam said two people could eat a whole quart of peaches before they spoiled. They canned beef, sausage, and little chunks of ham, all in pint jars that looked so cute, Lizzie found herself wanting to be married and making supper of her own.*
>
> WHEN STRAWBERRIES BLOOM

Sweet Dill Pickles

Makes 7-8 quarts
Prep Time: 2 hours
Cooking Time: 5 minutes • *Standing Time: 24 hours*

8 quarts
cucumbers

Brine
9 cups water
3 cups vinegar
3 Tbsp. salt
1 Tbsp. turmeric
½ cup kosher
dill pickle mix

1. Slice cucumbers into ½"-thick slices and place in jars.

2. Mix together brine ingredients in a large stockpot.

3. Bring to a boil.

4. Pour hot brine over cucumbers in jars, allowing 1" of headspace in each jar.

5. Follow "Canning Tips for Pickles" instruction on page 270, beginning with Step 5.

NOTE THIS IMPORTANT VARIATION TO STEP 10:

Boil for only 5 minutes.

Banana Pickles

Makes 4-5 quarts
Prep Time: 45-60 minutes
Cooking Time: 10 minutes • Standing Time: 24 hours

4 quarts cucumbers

Brine

2 cups vinegar

1 cup water

3 cups sugar

1 tsp. salt

1 tsp. celery salt

1 tsp. turmeric

1 tsp. mustard seed

1. Peel cucumbers and cut lengthwise.

2. Remove seeds.

3. Place cucumbers upright in quart jars.

4. Mix together ingredients for brine in a stockpot.

5. Bring to a boil.

6. Pour hot brine over cucumbers in jars, allowing 1" of headspace in each jar.

7. Follow "Canning Tips for Pickles" instructions on page 270, beginning with Step 5.

"Pickles!" Jason said loudly.
"Your sandwich is too dry, isn't it?" Lizzie grinned at him.
"No, 'course not. I'm just hungry for a pickle."
"How did it feel to have Lizzie for a teacher?" Mam asked.
Jason's mouth was stuffed with pickles, so he nodded his head before bending it to eat the other half of his sandwich in one bite.

WHEN STRAWBERRIES BLOOM

Pickled Red Beets

Makes 4-6 quarts
Prep Time: 2 hours
Cooking Time: 15-20 minutes • *Standing Time: 24 hours*

20 medium red beets
5-6 cups water
2 cups red beet juice
2 cups sugar
1 cup vinegar
1 Tbsp. salt

1. Cut off leaves and tops of fresh red beets, but leave enough of the base of the tops so that beets don't bleed. Do not cut off root ends.

2. Scrub well and place into large stockpot.

3. Add 5-6 cups of water.

4. Cook, covered, until almost soft.

5. Drain, reserving 2 cups of juice.

6. In separate bowl, mix together reserved juice, sugar, vinegar, and salt.

7. Boil for 3 minutes.

8. When beets are cool, cut off remaining top and roots.

9. Peel and cut into bite-sized pieces.

10. Place cut beets in quart or pint jars.

11. Pour juice over beets, allowing 1" of headspace in each jar.

12. Follow "Canning Tips for Pickles" instructions on page 270, beginning with Step 5.

NOTE THIS IMPORTANT VARIATION TO STEP 10:

Boil beets for 15-20 minutes.

TIP:

The easiest way to peel a beet is to use your hands to gently squeeze off the peel.

Canned Peaches

Makes 8 pints or 4 quarts
Prep Time: 1 hour
Cooking Time: 25 minutes • Standing Time: 24 hours

8-12 pounds peaches
4¼ cups sugar
4¼-5 cups water

1. Wash, pit, and peel peaches.

2. Cut peaches in half or in slices.

3. Place peaches in jars. If using peaches cut in half, make sure cavity faces downward in jar.

4. To prepare syrup, boil sugar and water in a stockpot, stirring and cooking just until sugar is dissolved.

5. Pour syrup over peaches, filling jars to within 1" of top.

6. Wipe rims of jars and put lids and rings on.

7. Place jars in canner. Water should not come above rings.

8. Boil for 25 minutes.

9. Remove from canner and let stand for 24 hours.

10. After 24 hours, check that all jars have sealed. Then remove rings and store. (Contents of jars that have not sealed should be discarded.)

TIP:

Prepare 1-1½ cups of syrup for each quart of fruit.

> *Mary was slicing a chocolate cake and topping each piece with home-canned peaches. Lizzie desperately wanted a large piece of cake soaked with sweet peach juice like she ate at home, but she was too embarrassed to eat that much in front of Daniel. She wasn't exactly thin, but she was trying. She certainly didn't want it to look as if she over-ate.*
>
> RUNNING AROUND
> (AND SUCH)

Canned Pears

Prep Time: 1 hour
Cooking Time: 25 minutes • *Standing Time: 24 hours*

8-12 pounds ripe, firm pears

3¼ cups sugar

5 cups water

1. Wash and peel pears. Remove cores and stem ends.

2. Cut into halves or slices.

3. Place pears in jars within 1" of rim. If using pears cut in half, put cavity side down in jars.

4. Prepare syrup by boiling sugar and water in a stockpot, stirring and cooking just until sugar is dissolved.

5. Pour syrup over pears.

6. Wipe rims of jars and put on lids and rings.

7. Place jars in canner with water just reaching rings.

8. Boil for 25 minutes.

9. Remove from canner and let stand for 24 hours.

10. After 24 hours, check that all jars have sealed. Then remove rings and store. (Contents of jars that have not sealed should be discarded.)

TIPS:

1. Bartlett pears are best for canning.

2. Allow 1-1½ cups syrup for each quart of fruit.

> *While the couples were changing their clothes, their helpers had set the bridal table with Emma's fancy tablecloths, her fine white china embellished with tiny garlands of flowers, the pitcher and glasses Joshua had given her, and the pretty silverware she had received from him, as well. Lizzie was even more excited by the food in front of them—bowls of fruit, cut-glass cake stands holding decorated wedding cakes, parfait glasses filled with a creamy gelatin dessert, and all kinds of other classy-looking dishes and food. It was a beautiful table with Joshua on one side and Emma on the other, both happier than Lizzie had ever seen them.*
>
> WHEN STRAWBERRIES BLOOM

Applesauce

Makes 8 pints or 4 quarts
Prep Time: 1½ hours
Cooking Time in canner: 20 minutes • Standing Time: 24 hours

12 pounds apples of
your choice

water

3 cups sugar, more or
less, depending on the
variety of apple and
your taste preference

4 Tbsp. lemon
juice, more or less,
depending on the
variety of apple and
your taste preference

1. Wash apples.

2. Core and cut into quarters.
   Apples may or may not be
   peeled.

3. Add water to stainless steel
   kettle, approximately 1"-2"
   deep.

4. Boil apples in kettle over
   medium-high heat. Stir up
   from bottom frequently to
   prevent apples from sticking.

5. Reduce heat and cook until
   apples are medium soft.

6. Remove from heat.

7. Using a Victorio strainer or
   food processor with metal
   blades, puree cooked apples
   until smooth.

8. Add sugar and lemon juice to
   taste. Spoon hot applesauce
   into jars.

9. Wipe rims of jars and put on lids and rings.

10. Place jars in canner. Add water up to rims of jars.

11. Boil for 20 minutes.

12. Remove from canner and allow to sit for 24 hours.

13. After 24 hours, check that all jars are sealed; then remove rings and store. (Contents of jars that have not sealed should be discarded.)

TIP:

Peeling apples makes applesauce lighter in color.

Ham sandwiches, applesauce, carrots and dip, and chocolate pudding rounded out the Valentine's Day menu. Lizzie would supply the paper plates and cups and choose all the games.

Lizzie sat at her desk while the children planned, writing notes to the mothers explaining what their children should bring for the party. The pupils each folded Lizzie's notes and stored them carefully in their lunchboxes.

Valentine's Day was such a big event in the one-room schoolhouse, even if the upper-grade boys pretended to hate it.

BIG DECISIONS

Homemade Grape Juice Concentrate

Makes 2 quarts
Prep Time: 1½ hours
Draining Time: 24 hours • Cooking Time: 45 minutes

5½-6 pounds
Concord grapes

2 cups water

1½ cups sugar, *divided*

1. Wash grapes and take off stems.

2. Place grapes in very large kettle with water.

3. Cover. Bring to boil.

4. Reduce heat. Cook over medium heat for 30 minutes.

5. Remove from heat. Pour grapes into cheese-cloth-lined bowls.

6. Allow grapes to drain for 24 hours in the fridge.

7. Place juice in stockpot. Stir in 1 cup sugar. Taste. Add more sugar if you wish.

8. Bring juice to boil.

9. Pour juice into hot jars, allowing ½" headspace.

10. Follow Canning Tips on page 270, beginning with Step 5.

11. After water in canner comes to a boil, cook for 10-15 minutes.

12. To serve, mix grape juice concentrate with water and sugar to taste. Serve chilled.

Mrs. Fisher served a snack of pretzels and cheese, leftover snitz pie, and grape juice after the singing was over. Lizzie and her friends laughed and talked with the parents easily. In this small budding community, the two generations had a close relationship.

WHEN STRAWBERRIES BLOOM

Grape Jelly

Makes 7 8-oz. jars
Prep Time: 5 minutes
Cooking Time: 15 minutes • Standing Time: 24 hours

5 cups unsweetened
grape juice

1¾-oz. pkg. powdered
fruit pectin

6 cups sugar

1. Pour juice into large saucepan.

2. Over medium heat, whisk pectin into juice until dissolved.

3. Bring mixture to full boil over high heat, stirring often.

4. Add sugar and return to full, rolling boil.

5. Boil hard for 1 minute, stirring constantly.

6. Remove from heat and skim off foam.

7. Pour hot jelly into jars, filling to ¼"-½" of the top.

8. Wipe rims and put on lids and rings.

9. Place jars in canner, completely covering with water.

10. Boil for 10 minutes.

11. Remove jars from canner and allow to cool for 24 hours. Do not remove rings.

12. After 24 hours, check that all jars have sealed. Then remove rings and store. (Contents of jars that have not sealed should be discarded.)

VARIATION:

With sweetened grape juice, use 4½ cups of sugar instead of 6.

> *"But…but…," Mam spluttered. Then she did what she sometimes did when she was at a loss for words. She scolded. Clicking the gas burner lower, a bit more forcefully than was absolutely necessary, she said angrily, "Now see, Mandy, you made me burn these eggs. Lizzie, don't just stand there doing nothing. Get the juice poured. There's no jelly on the table."*
>
> *The subject was closed until Dat had finished his breakfast. Then Mam brought it into the open, abruptly and unexpectedly.*
>
> *"Mandy says John wants to marry her in March."*
>
> BIG DECISIONS

Peach Jelly

Makes 5 8-oz. jars
Prep Time: 30 minutes • Draining Time: 2-8 hours, or overnight
Cooking Time: 20-25 minutes • Standing Time: 24 hours

3 lbs. fresh peaches,
or enough to
extract 3 cups
peach juice

water

½ cup lemon juice

1¾-oz. pkg.
powdered fruit
pectin

5 cups sugar

1. Wash, peel, and pit peaches. Cut into quarters.

2. Place peaches in large saucepan.

3. Add ½ cup water for each pound of peaches.

4. Bring to boil over high heat, stirring often.

5. Reduce heat and boil gently for 20 minutes or until peaches are soft. Occasionally stir and crush peaches.

6. Pour peaches into cheesecloth placed in a strainer. Allow to drain 2-8 hours or overnight, collecting 3 cups peach juice.

7. Pour 3 cups peach juice and lemon juice into large saucepan.

8. Whisk pectin into juice until dissolved.

9. Bring mixture to full boil over high heat, stirring often.

10. Add sugar and return to full, rolling boil.

11. Boil hard for 1 minute, stirring constantly.

12. Remove from heat and skim off foam.

13. Pour hot jelly into jars, filling to ¼"-½" of top.

14. Wipe rims and put on lids and rings.

15. Place jars in canner, completely covering with water.

16. Boil for 10 minutes.

17. Remove jars from canner and allow to cool for 24 hours. Do not remove rings.

18. After 24 hours, check that all jars have sealed. Then remove rings and store. (Contents of jars that have not sealed should be discarded.)

TIP:

Three medium-sized peaches weight about 1 pound.

Cold macaroni salad and thick slices of homemade bread with butter and peach jam completed their meal.

Everything tasted wonderful, even the macaroni salad.

RUNNING
AROUND
(AND SUCH)

Strawberry Jelly

Makes 5 8-oz. jars

Prep Time: 30 minutes • Draining Time: 2-8 hours, or overnight
Cooking Time: 20-25 minutes • Standing Time: 24 hours

3 cups fresh
strawberries

½ cup water

2 Tbsp. lemon
juice

1¾-oz. pkg.
fruit pectin

4½ cups sugar

1. Wash berries, removing stems. Slice.

2. Put sliced berries in saucepan with ½ cup water.

3. Bring berries to a boil, stirring often.

4. Reduce heat and boil 5-10 minutes, crushing berries lightly.

5. Place berries into cheesecloth in strainer and allow to drain for 2-8 hours or overnight into bowl. Do not press down on strawberries; that may make the jelly cloudy.

6. Pour juice from strawberries and lemon juice into large saucepan.

7. Whisk pectin into juice until dissolved.

8. Bring mixture to full boil over high heat, stirring often.

9. Add sugar and return to full, rolling boil.

10. Boil hard for 1 minute, stirring constantly.

11. Remove from heat and skim off foam.

12. Pour hot jelly into jars, filling to ¼"-½" of top.

13. Wipe rims and put on lids and rings.

14. Place jars in canner, completely covering with water.

15. Boil for 10 minutes.

16. Remove jars from canner and allow to cool for 24 hours. Do not remove rings.

17. After 24 hours, check that all jars have sealed. Then remove rings and store.

> *Lizzie sighed happily as she spread strawberry jam on a crisp piece of toast.*
>
> **WHEN STRAWBERRIES BLOOM**

Tomato Juice

Makes 1 quart
Prep Time: 45 minutes
Cooking Time: 40 minutes • *Standing Time: 24 hours*

3-3¼ pounds tomatoes for 1 quart tomato juice

2 Tbsp. lemon juice, *or* ½ tsp. citric acid, for 1 quart tomato juice

salt, *optional*

1. Wash tomatoes, removing stems and any spots.

2. Pour 1" water in large, stainless steel kettle.

3. Add tomatoes.

4. Boil gently until tomatoes are soft and pulpy.

5. Press hot tomatoes through Victorio strainer, fine sieve, or food mill.

6. Discard seeds and skins.

7. Pour hot tomato juice into jars.

8. Add lemon juice and salt if you wish.

9. Wipe rims of jars and put on lids and rings.

10. Place jars in canner with water up to rings.

11. Boil 40 minutes.

12. Remove from canner and let stand for 24 hours.

13. After 24 hours, check that all jars have sealed. Then remove rings and store. (Contents of jars that have not sealed should be discarded.)

TIP:

If tomatoes are large, cut in half.

Plain Tomato Sauce

Makes 7 quarts
Prep Time: 30 minutes
Cooking Time: 2¾ hours – 3¾ hours • *Standing Time: 24 hours*

35 pounds of tomatoes for thin tomato sauce

46 pounds of tomatoes for thick tomato sauce

2 Tbsp. lemon juice *or* ½ tsp. citric acid for 1 quart tomato juice

1. Follow directions for making Tomato Juice (p. 292) through Step 6 to make tomato sauce.

2. When tomatoes are juiced and seeded, pour juice into large, stainless steel kettle.

3. Bring juice to boiling.

4. Reduce heat to medium-high and boil until juice is reduced to sauce.

5. Put lemon juice in bottom of jars.

6. Add tomato sauce to jars within 1" of top.

7. Wipe rims and put on lids and rings.

8. Place water in canner and bring to a boil.

Canning Recipes

9. Carefully place jars into canner of boiling water. Water should reach the bottoms of the jar rings, but never go over the lids.

10. Make sure water is boiling before timing the cooking.

11. Jars must boil 40 minutes.

12. After jars have boiled 40 minutes, turn burner off.

13. Using a jar lifter, remove jars from hot water.

14. Keeping rings on jars, let rest 24 hours.

15. After 24 hours, remove rings and make sure all lids have sealed. An unsealed jar can be refrigerated for several days. After that, discard contents of jar.

TIP:

Plum or Roma tomatoes are best for tomato sauce.

> *Lizzie said hello to everyone before helping herself to a slice of the thick homemade pizza. It was one of the most delicious things she had ever eaten. The crust was thick and springy, with hot tomato sauce and cheese melting off the sides. Sausage and pepperoni sat on top of the melting cheese.*
>
> WHEN STRAWBERRIES BLOOM

Pizza Sauce

Makes 4 pints
Prep Time: 1 hour for purée • Cooking Time: 45 minutes

13 cups fresh
tomato sauce
½ cup lemon juice
2 tsp. dried oregano
1 tsp. black pepper
1 tsp. salt
1½ tsp. garlic powder

1. Follow directions for making Plain Tomato Sauce (p. 294) through Step 4.

2. Pour tomato puree into large stainless steel saucepan.

3. Stir in lemon juice, oregano, black pepper, salt, and garlic powder.

4. Boil 15 minutes, or until sauce has reached preferred consistency.

5. Remove from heat and pour into jars within 1" of top.

6. Wipe rims of jars and add lids and rings.

7. Place water in canner and bring to a boil.

8. Carefully place jars into canner of boiling water. Water should reach the bottoms of the jar rings, but never go over the lids.

Canning Recipes

9. Make sure water is boiling before timing the cooking.

10. Jars must boil 35 minutes after coming to a boil.

11. After jars have boiled 35 minutes, turn burner off.

12. Using a jar lifter, remove jars from hot water.

13. Keeping rings on jars, let rest 24 hours.

14. After 24 hours, remove rings and make sure all lids have sealed. An unsealed jar can be refrigerated for several days. After that, discard contents of jar.

TIP:

Add additional seasonings to suit your taste—basil and onion salt, for example—in Step 3.

> *Inside the house, Mrs. King had all kinds of delicious food for the skaters, which helped ease Lizzie's sense of disappointment about leaving the pond. The dining room table was filled with big thick slices of homemade pizza piled high with cheese and browned ground beef, root beer in glass mugs, crackers, pretzels and potato chips, and warm chocolate chip cookies for dessert.*
>
> RUNNING AROUND (AND SUCH)

The law of the Lord is perfect,

converting the soul:

the testimony of the LORD is
    sure,

making wise the simple…

More to be desired are they than
    gold,

yea, than much fine gold:

sweeter also than honey and the
    honeycomb.

PSALM 19:7-10

Recipe List

Index of Ingredients and Food Categories

A

Apples
Apple Crumb Pie, 200
Apple Salad, 170
Applesauce, 282
Schnitz Pie, 212

B

Bananas
Apple Salad, 170
Banana Nut Bread, 25
Banana Pudding, 246

Barbecue
Barbecued Beans, 182
Barbecued Chicken Sandwiches, 138
Barbecued Green Beans, 179
Barbecued Ham Sandwiches, 140
Beef Barbecue Sandwiches, 144

Beans
Barbecued Beans, 182
Ham and Bean Soup, 124
Hamburger Veggie Soup, 128

Beef, Dried
Creamed Dried Beef, 42

Beef, Ground
Beef and Potato Loaf, 89
Beef Barbecue Sandwiches, 144
Camper's Special, 98
Cheeseburgers, 142
Cheeseburger Soup, 125
Hamburger Casserole, 94
Hamburger Gravy, 96
Hamburger Veggie Soup, 128
Hot Roast Hamburger, 92
Macaroni and Hamburger Casserole, 100
Meat Loaf, 90
Pizza Casserole, 102
Poor Man's Steak, 103
Pour Pizza, 104

Pizza Sauce, 296
Plain Tomato Sauce, 294
Strawberry Jelly, 290
Sweet Dill Pickles, 274
Tomato Juice, 292

Carrots
Baked Beef Stew, 88
Beef Vegetable Soup, 126
Carrot-Raisin Salad, 160
Cheeseburger Soup, 125
Chicken Pie, 70
Chicken Stew, 66
Creamy Cole Slaw, 165
Hot Roast Hamburger, 92
Layered Green Salad, 162
Macaroni Salad, 168
Ohio Filling, 80
Potato Soup, 132

Casseroles
Breakfast Casserole, 40
Chicken Casserole, 72
Green Bean and Sausage
    Casserole, 110
Green Bean Casserole, 180
Hamburger Casserole, 94
Macaroni and Hamburger
    Casserole, 100
Pizza Casserole, 102
Sausage Potato Casserole, 112
Sweet Potato Casserole, 194
Zucchini Casserole, 196

Cauliflower
Broccoli and Cauliflower Salad,
    156

Celery
Beef Vegetable Soup, 126
Carrot-Raisin Salad, 160
Cheeseburger Soup, 125
Chicken Corn Soup, 120
Chicken Pie, 70
Chicken Salad Sandwiches, 150
Cole Slaw, 164
Cooked Celery, 197

Hamburger Veggie Soup, 128
Layered Green Salad, 162
Macaroni Salad, 168
Ohio Filling, 80
Potato Salad, 166
Roasht or Chicken Filling, 78
Roast Turkey, 82

Cheese
Breakfast Casserole, 40
Cheeseburgers, 142
Chicken Gumbo, 76
Chicken Noodle Bake, 74
Cream of Tuna Soup, 130
Floating Islands, 118
Hot Dog Surprise, 151
Layered Green Salad, 162
Macaroni and Hamburger
    Casserole, 100
Pour Pizza, 104
Saturday Night Sandwiches, 146
Sausage Potato Casserole, 112
Scalloped Potatoes, 188
Turkey Bake, 84
Zucchini Casserole, 196

Cheese, American
Baked Macaroni and Cheese, 116
Cheese Spread, 30

Cheese, Cheddar
Baked Macaroni and Cheese, 116
Green Bean and Sausage
    Casserole, 110

Cheese, Mozzarella
Pizza Casserole, 102

Cheese, Velveeta
Cheeseburger Soup, 125
Hot Bologna and Cheese
    Sandwiches, 148
Potluck Potatoes, 186
Toasted Cheese Sandwiches, 152

Cherries, Maraschino
Old-Fashioned Baked Ham, 108

> *Give us this day
> our daily
> bread.*
> MATTHEW 6:11

*O taste and
see that the
LORD is
good:*

*blessed is the man
that trusteth
in him.*

PSALM 34:8

Gelatin
Christmas Salad, 172
Jello Mold, 174

Ginger
Molasses Cookies, 230

Grapes
Homemade Grape Juice
Concentrate, 284

Gravy
Chicken or Beef Gravy, 77
Hamburger Gravy, 96
Sausage Gravy, 44
Tomato Gravy, 45

Green Beans
Barbecued Green Beans, 179
Beef Vegetable Soup, 126
Chicken Casserole, 72
Green Bean and Sausage
Casserole, 110
Green Bean Casserole, 180
Hamburger Casserole, 94
Ham, Green Beans, and Potato
Stew, 122

Jelly
Grape Jelly, 286
Peach Jelly, 288
Strawberry Jelly, 290

L

Lard
Becky Zook Bread, 8
Onion Patties, 193
Whole Wheat Bread, 12

Lemons
Lemonade, 260

Lettuce
Christmas Salad, 172
Layered Green Salad, 162
Lettuce with Cream Dressing,
158

M

Marshmallow Crème
Church Peanut Butter
Marshmallow Spread, 28

Marshmallows
Hot Chocolate Mix, 267

H

Honey
Quick Cinnamon Rolls, 20
Whole Wheat Bread, 12

R

S

*Thou preparest a
table before
me*

*in the presence of
mine enemies:*

*thou anointest my
head with oil;*

*my cup runneth
over.*

PSALM 23:5

V

Vegetable Juice
Baked Beef Stew, 88

W

Walnuts
Butterscotch Nut Cookies, 228
Christmas Cake, 236

Whipped Topping
Banana Pudding, 246
Chocolate Pie, 214
Christmas Salad, 172
Creamy Jelly Roll Topping, 245
Date Pudding, 250
Jello Mold, 174
Vanilla Cornstarch Pudding, 248

Whipping Cream
French Chocolate, 266

Whoopie Pies
Chocolate Whoopie Pies, 218
Pumpkin Whoopie Pies, 221
Whoopie Pie Filling, 220

Z

Zucchini
Zucchini Bread, 27
Zucchini Casserole, 196

Start each day with

A fresh beginning;

As if this whole world

Was made anew.

MOTTO FROM AN
AMISH SCHOOL IN
PENNSYLVANIA

About The Authors

Linda Byler grew up Amish and is an active member of the Amish church today. Growing up, Linda loved to read and write. In fact, she still does. She is the author of *Running Around (and Such)*, the first novel in the "Lizzie Searches for Love" series, of *When Strawberries Bloom*, the second novel in that series, and of *Big Decisions*, the third book in the series.

The recipes in *Lizzie's Amish Cookbook* were selected by Linda Byler's daughter, Laura Ann Lapp, who lives in the same Amish community as her parents. Laura, who enjoys cooking and gardening, and her husband are the parents of three sons. Laura spent hours with her grandmother, Anna Kauffman (Linda Byler's mother), poring over well-worn cookbooks together to choose the best of Amish cooking – just like Lizzie enjoyed!

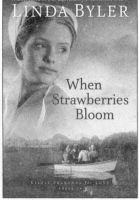

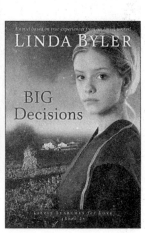